Anything Dr Michael Eaton [...] his treatment of the Sermon [...] superior, to anything written [...] have to read long and hard to [...] tion of a particular verse; it emerges quickly, simply and clearly and always in an edifying manner. I have used it in preparation for my own preaching on the subject; I wouldn't proceed without it! No church leader or layman should be without it now that it is available for a wider circulation.

R T Kendall,
Westminster Chapel
London

THE WAY THAT LEADS TO LIFE

Preaching Through
the Sermon on the Mount

Michael Eaton

Christian Focus

Christian Focus Publications publishes biblically-accurate books for adults and children. The books in the adult range are published in three imprints.

Christian Heritage contains classic writings from the past.

Christian Focus contains popular works including biographies, commentaries, doctrine, and Christian living.

Mentor focuses on books written at a level suitable for Bible College and seminary students, pastors, and others; the imprint includes commentaries, doctrinal studies, examination of current issues, and church history.

For a free catalogue of all our titles, please write to
Christian Focus Publications,
Geanies House, Fearn,
Ross-shire, IV20 1TW, Great Britain

For details of our titles visit us on our web site
http://www.christianfocus.com

© Michael Eaton
ISBN 1 85792 339 1

Published in 1999
by
Christian Focus Publications,
Geanies House, Fearn, Ross-shire,
IV20 1TW, Great Britain.

Contents

Preface

The Sermon on the Mount is perhaps the greatest, the most searching, the most challenging part of the Bible. When I came to preach on it again recently I approached it with great awe and wonder. The more I read it, the more I preach on it, the more awe-inspiring it becomes. How any of us ever dare preach on it I do not know, but we have to do so! I have preached through the Sermon on the Mount five times, in Lusaka, in Nairobi, in Johannesburg, over the radio via Trans World Radio, and then in West Kenya more recently as I was writing these chapters. I think I have grown in my understanding of it and my last exposition was certainly much better than my first exposition of it.

The Sermon on the Mount is never easy to write about. Who could ever write about these words of Jesus without feeling hypocritical? No one is an expert when it comes to living the Sermon on the Mount. At the moment I read bits of my own little book almost every day. I need it! Of all the books I have written, none has been so valuable to my own life as this one. It is hardly possible to write on the Sermon on the Mount without being convicted of one's own sinfulness. Never is the blood of Jesus Christ more needed!

This little volume is part of a number of books that I hope to write on Matthew's Gospel. In the *Preaching Through the Bible* series for Sovereign World it will take two volumes to go through Matthew, but I felt that the

Sermon on the Mount needed special attention and that is the explanation of this volume. It is similar in style to the *Preaching Through the Bible* books, but more detailed. I have an idea Satan was not enjoying my writing this little book. I seemed to have peculiar difficulties confronting me every time I tried to write on this passage of Scripture. The day I started writing I had just discovered that a lifetime's recordings of my preaching had somehow got mislaid – including two attempts at preaching on the Sermon on the Mount. I had wanted simply to transcribe my preaching, but that was not possible. The missing recordings were partly replaced but I distinctly had the feeling that Satan had stolen the first lot!

My aims and style of writing in this book are much the same as in most other writings of mine.

(i) They are somewhat culture-free. Of course I realize that there is no such thing as being culture-free! The English language itself is a culture! Kenyan friends of mine who use English as their home language are somewhat English in their ways and mannerisms! If I visit a rural village in Kenya and speak in a mixture of English and Swahili with some local vernacular phrases thrown in, my mannerisms change as well as my language. Even the way I eat becomes different! What I mean by 'somewhat culture-free' is this: it is possible to write books in English that have rather less heavily European/Western overtones and stories. If I were to put stories and illustrations in my books they would related to Africa. When I preach in City Hall, Nairobi, my illustrations are all local – but I write for a wider audience. I have spent virtually all my working life in Africa and the congregations I speak to generally do not have a detailed knowledge of Europe or North America. In such a situation I do not use European illustrations.

(ii) All my books are actually 'academic' books and have the same sort of research behind them as my published academic works. My M.Th. thesis (*The Baptism with the Spirit*..., IVP, now out of print), my D.Th. thesis (*A Theology of Encouragement*, Paternoster) and my contribution to the Tyndale Commentaries (*Ecclesiastes*) are visibly academic. The rest are invisibly academic – but the amount of research done is much the same. I work through the journals and academic theses constantly. I just reckon that ordinary people don't like footnotes or academic jargon and I write for ordinary people – most of the time.

So in my mind what you have here is an academic work on the Sermon on the Mount, but no one else is likely to take it that way since it has few footnotes and no laying out of research. What is found here is not the research but the results and the conclusions that I have come to. I can report that (although I have not actually made much use of them in the writing of these pages) the expositions that have meant most to me over the years are those by A.W. Pink, John Brown (*Discourses and Sayings of Our Lord*), D.M. Lloyd-Jones, Don Carson and J.R.W. Stott. More recently I have profited from Guelich's work, *The Sermon on the Mount* (Word, 1982). Although it is more historical and 'critical' in its style, it is a mine of information.

(iii) I am not fussy about 'inclusive language' although I do sometimes shape the English language in the interests of half the human race. Sentences like 'It is as if someone is praying at night that they will have enough to live on the next day!' – although mildly ungrammatical – are my contribution to the 'inclusive language' debate. 'They' means 'he or she'.

As always, I am grateful to my family for their continued support of my preaching; and the friends at the Chrisco Fellowship of Churches in Nairobi continue to be a source of encouragement to me in my preaching and writing. To many wonderful people who were with me in West Kenya and were colleagues and friends during the preaching and writing of these chapters in 1998 I am most grateful: Alice Anyango from Nairobi and her brother Pastor Stephen Onyango, Salome Odero from Maseno, Pastor Abiud Kimathi and his wife Mary Kimathi in the Kisumu Chrisco Church, Sally Musua who was studying in Maseno University, Emma Nviri from Nairobi Miracle centre, Pastor Eliud from Sega and his wife Eunice; and Judith Oswego also from Sega and once a worshipper at my old church, the Nairobi Baptist Church, plus the congregations at Maseno Miracle Centre and Kisumu Chrisco Church; and (not least) the Okwaras and Onyangos of Maseno University in whose homes we stayed. May these chapters bring back happy memories of some good days together a few yards from the equator.

In these pages I provide my own translation of the biblical text and of early Christian writers.

1. Introducing the Sermon on the Mount
(Matthew 5:1-2)

The 'Sermon on the Mount' is the popular name for a block of teaching recorded in Matthew's Gospel, chapters 5 to 7. Early on in his ministry in Galilee, Jesus gave to his disciples some concentrated teaching concerning the godly life that he expected his disciples to live. Matthew implies that it was given on one particular occasion but it is not necessary to think that it was one 'sermon'. More likely, Matthew chapters 5 to 7 are an abridged statement of the teaching that he gave during an entire day or over the course of several days. It is obviously a summary. Luke has an even shorter summary in Luke 6:20-49. I have a sound-recording of someone reading Matthew's version. It takes about fourteen minutes to read aloud.

Matthew obviously claims that the preaching recorded in Matthew 5:3-7:27 was a definite block of teaching given on a single occasion. The idea that the Sermon is Matthew's creation and that Matthew strung together sayings and teachings from different parts of Jesus' life is contradicted by 7:28-8:1. Scholars who hold such views begin by rejecting the claims of Matthew's Gospel, and then try to work out what really happened! But Matthew's Gospel is itself the evidence, and we should follow the only evidence that we have. Matthew is clearly claiming that everything in 5:3-7:27 is one unit of Jesus' teaching, given on a definite occasion. This teaching on this particular occasion amazed the crowds of Jesus' disciples.

The first phase of Jesus' Galilean ministry (Mark 1:14-3:6; Luke 4:14-6:11) came to a climax when Jesus became

11

popular, and yet was in danger of being killed by the Pharisees (Mark 3:6; Luke 6:11). This perhaps took place in the early part of AD 31. Jesus probably went to the Passover celebrations in 31. About this time a second phase of Jesus' Galilean ministry began (Mark 3:7-6:6; Luke 6:12-8:56). It perhaps takes place in the middle of 31. (Some think the dates are three years earlier). People came from all over the country to hear Jesus, from as far as Idumea in the south, from as far as Tyre and Sidon in the north (Mark 3:7-12). At this point Jesus chooses some higher ground among the hills to the north of the sea of Galilee. It is a less populated area and Jesus goes there to pray (Luke 6:12), to choose twelve disciples (Mark 3:13-19; Luke 6:12-16), to heal the sicknesses of his followers (Luke 6:17-19) and to teach them (Luke 6:20-49). Jesus' ministry to his disciples presumably takes place at a part of hillside where there is a level place or a natural auditorium. There he preaches the famous 'Sermon on the Mount', presumably a block of teaching conducted over several days rather than a single meeting with a single sermon.

This 'Sermon on the Mount' is one of many passages of Scripture giving us some of the detailed requirements of the godly life. There are many such passages in the New Testament, some emphasizing this aspect of the godly life, some emphasizing another aspect. Early on in his ministry in Galilee, Jesus called his closer disciples to 'enter into life' by the way in which they lived in dependence on him and on his kingdom.

Matthew begins by giving us the picture of how Jesus came to give this teaching. *But seeing the multitudes, he went up into the hill country. And when he had sat down his disciples came to him* (5:1). *And he opened his mouth and taught them* (5:2). *Blessed are the poor in spirit...* (5:3). We see that the Sermon on the Mount is addressed to disciples. This is quite important for us and affects our interpretation. It is emphasized in 5:1: 'Seeing the multitudes, he went up into the hill country ... his disciples came ... and he taught them...'. It seems that there was a time in Jesus ministry when crowds were following him. Seeing them, Jesus deliberately withdrew himself from places where he could be easily reached and went somewhere slightly inconvenient in the hill-country to the north of the Sea of Galilee. It would have had the effect of leaving aside the uncommitted and giving opportunity for something special for those who were more loyal to him. This is confirmed when we see exactly at what stage this event happened in the life of Jesus. A study of the first three gospels reveals to us that on the same occasion, Jesus went to the hill country, spent one particular night in prayer, in the next morning chose his twelve apostles and spoke of their going out to extend his ministry. It was on this occasion that Jesus gave 'the Sermon on the Mount'. It was not an evangelistic message but a challenge to Jesus' closest followers, many of them just about to set out on a lifetime of ministry. People like Peter and James were gripped by it and never forgot it.

Another thing that confirms this point is that when the disciples are addressed it is taken for granted that they are truly Jesus' disciples. 'You are the light of the world... the salt of the earth.' This sermon was not given to enemies or uncertain half-disciples. The original hearers of this preaching were the salt of the earth and the light of the world. This fact affects our interpretation at points.

This means that the Sermon on the Mount is not exactly evangelistic. Some have thought that its purpose is to convict us of sin and to drive us to faith in Jesus – like an evangelistic sermon. There is something to be said for this, for Christians need 'the evangelistic message' as well as the unsaved. We never get beyond the point of needing to be driven back to the grace of God. We never get to the point where we do not need the blood of Jesus Christ. Yet, despite this fact, the Sermon is not evangelism for unbelieving outsiders. It does not exactly declare the good news in the way that is found in Matthew 11:28-30. It is not an evangelistic sermon like those of the book of Acts.

The way in which the Sermon is presented also means that the Sermon on the Mount was never intended to be a general law for society. This is even more obvious. Many of the particular injunctions could never be implemented by a magistrate, and would be entirely beyond the 'natural man' (to use Paul's phrase in 1 Cor. 2:14). They were not addressed to anyone and everyone. 'What do you do more than others?' Jesus asked his disciples, and in so doing implied he was addressing them, not the 'others'. Jesus explicitly took his disciples away from the common run of humanity and gave them teaching which he was not giving others. It is not that the Sermon is some kind of secret teaching; but it is designed for disciples, it is not designed for people in general.

The Sermon is not 'law' at all. True, we could call it 'the law of Christ' (using the phrase of Gal. 6:2) but it is not 'law' in the normal sense of that term. Some of its commands are not intended to be taken literally. The early church father Origen literally emasculated himself in supposed obedience to Matthew 5:29, 30 ('it is better that you lose one of your members') but he was surely mistaken in doing so – and physical deformity does not hinder sin! We are not literally to give to every beggar that asks us – perhaps to purchase his next dose of drugs. We only have one 'other cheek' to turn which does not fit 'seventy times seven' mentioned elsewhere! It all shows that the instructions of the Sermon are at points parabolic rather than strictly literal. They deal with the spirit more than coming to us as a law-code.

The Sermon is not an exposition of the Law of Moses, although it could be said to be an exposition of the *fulfilment* of the Law of Moses – which is a different thing. The Sermon ignores thousands of the requirements of the law (circumcision, holy days, the tabernacle, regulations about slaves, and so on). It upgrades some aspects of the law into a higher spirituality. It *abolishes* other aspects of the law altogether, withdrawing something that was permitted (easy divorce), discouraging something that was commanded (oath-taking), and urging things that were never mentioned by the law (praying for enemies). The law of Moses *foreshadowed* a higher righteousness, and the Sermon is an exposition of the fulfilment of the law rather than an exposition of the shadow. Jesus talked about 'fulfilling' the law and this is not precisely the same as maintaining the law.

The Sermon is a description of the kind of life that is to be lived by Jesus' disciples. Although it cannot be taken completely literally, yet Jesus clearly expected his disciples

15

to actually live in the way he commends and commands. Although no one will ever get to the point where he or she can say 'I keep the Sermon on the Mount', yet we are intended to start climbing this holy mountain, even if we only reach the top in heaven! The commands must not be limited to a few elite Christians who are following 'counsels of perfection' which others do not need. Nor is 'the Sermon' intended merely for a future dispensation. No doubt the Sermon shatters our self-confidence and leads us to repentance. At the same time it tells us to get up and start changing our lives to conform to the quality of life demanded by the teaching of Jesus.

A few points, developed in some detail, constitute Jesus' simple description of a godly life, addressed to his Jewish disciples. There might have been a slightly different emphasis if he had been speaking to Gentile believers who knew nothing of the Mosaic law, but since every Christian who reads his Bible knows about the Mosaic law, the words in 5:17-48 are as necessary for us as they were for these early Jewish disciples.

The Sermon begins with a basic description of the character of a disciple (5:3-16) and tells of how he or she fulfils the Mosaic law (5:17-48). The disciple lives in the sight of God (6:1-34) and without a judgmental attitude towards others (7:1-6). Supremely he or she must live prayerfully (7:7-11) and follow the practice of love (7:12) in the wisdom that consists of obeying the words of Jesus (7:13-27). I, for one, am embarrassed every time I look at this Sermon on the Mount. What high standards it holds before us. But Jesus died to purify for himself a people of his own who are zealous for good deeds. Jesus died that we might live the Sermon on the Mount. None of us have got to the top of the mountain – but it is time to start climbing.

2. The Christian's Humility (Matthew 5:3-5)

The Sermon begins with a basic description of the character of a disciple. Matthew 5:3-12 is commonly known as the beatitudes (although the sub-section extends to 5:16).

Blessed are the poor in spirit, said Jesus (5:3). 'Poverty' is when a person does not have sufficient good food to be able to stay healthy. It is when a person does not have adequate clothing to protect his dignity and his health against cold weather and rain. It is when a person does not have a shelter, a place to call 'home' in which to keep some private possessions.

A literally poor person is conscious of great need. He knows he does not have what others have. To be 'poor in spirit' is similar. It is to be conscious of need in relation to the things of God. When the 'poor in spirit' prays he says to God: 'Lord, I have nothing with which to commend myself to you, except Jesus whom you have given to me. I know that in myself I really am a failure in the life of righteousness. I can do all things through Jesus but I have often failed to be what you call me to be.' He or she is totally honest before God, and when he is totally honest he knows how selfish he is, how much he likes his own desires to get fulfilled. He knows what a long way he has to go if he is to get anywhere near being like Jesus.

The person who is 'poor in spirit' is wholly and utterly

17

dependent on God. When a really destitute person is in financial trouble there is often not much he can do except pray or beg! If there is a sickness or an unexpected bill, what can one do? In such a situation one is wholly dependent on the generosity of others. God has to work powerfully, or others have to help you in some way – or you perish!

So the 'poor in spirit' is utterly dependent on God. For righteousness. For spiritual power. For growth in godliness. For everything!

There is a connection between being financially poor and being 'poor in spirit'. 'You poor' (Luke 6:20) and 'poor in spirit' (Matthew) are two aspects of the same thing. Luke paraphrases Jesus' teaching more emphatically in a socio-economic manner. 'Blessed are you poor' is his summary of Jesus teaching. Jesus' original message was probably in Aramaic and, as I have noted before, it probably took all day or several days when it was originally given to the disciples. Matthew and Luke are just giving summaries. They emphasize different aspects of the teaching. A person who is 'poor in spirit' will always sympathize and identify with the socially poor. When Jesus spoke (in Luke's version) of 'you poor' he was referring to disciples who were financially poor and so were utterly dependent on Jesus. And he was referring also to those who identify with such people! The gospel is specially for the poor! God has chosen the poor (Jas. 2:5)! Those who are rich are welcome as long as they identify with the poor. The 'poor in spirit' is always at one with the financially poor even if he is not actually one of the financially poor.

I believe the most important phrase in the Sermon on

the Mount is this one. If we understand what it means to be 'poor in spirit' we shall understand the whole Sermon on the Mount.

Blessed are those that mourn ..., said Jesus (5:4). The blessing does not come upon the mourning in itself. It is not that Christians are only happy when they are miserable! Nor are we precisely being told to mourn (as is the case in Jas. 4:9). It is simply assumed that the disciples are grieving over something. Often it is said it is the grief we feel over our own sinfulness. This is part of it, but there is more to be said. It is clearly temporary; a change is about to come ('They shall be comforted'). Luke's summary of Jesus' Aramaic teaching is: 'Blessed are you that weep now, for you shall laugh' (Luke 6:21; see also Psa. 126:5-6). Mourning cannot be the whole story for the Christian, for Peter says that even now in this age before the Second Coming of Jesus, though we do not see Jesus, we rejoice with a joy that is unspeakable and full of glory (1 Pet. 1:8). In Matthew's Gospel it is said that God's people cannot mourn 'while the Bridegroom is with them' (9:15).

God's people rejoice because Jesus has come. They mourn because the kingdom has not come as fully as they would like. This 'mourning' is grief at the situation we find ourselves in. We, the righteous, suffer unjustly (see 5:10-12). The wicked prosper. God's will is not yet done on earth as it is done in heaven (see 6:10). And we ourselves are not as righteous as we would like to be in our own daily lives. Christians have mixed emotions as they face the spiritual situation they find themselves in. They are lamenting the fact that God's kingdom has not fully come either in the world or in themselves. Upon such

19

people – people who hunger and thirst for the righteousness that has not yet fully come – a benediction rests.

In the Christian life there is some sorrow before there is full joy. While we must be careful to guard against 'preparationism' (the heresy that says we have to prepare ourselves in some way before we can put our trust in Jesus Christ), yet for the believer there is often a grim side to life before there is the fulness of joy that comes from God. Of course, these 'mourners' are already believers. The grief is the result of what they know to be the truth. The grief is not preparation for faith.

These beatitudes are not exactly commands; they are more explanations. They are not precisely telling us to be poor and to mourn, but they are informing us that when we are conscious of our poverty, and when we are grieving that the world is not yet as it ought to be, and nor are we ourselves as we ought to be – upon such people the blessing of God rests.

Blessed are the meek, said Jesus (5:5). 'Meekness' is the absence of defensiveness. It is when we are able to leave our case and our cause in the hands of God; we are happy to let God set the record straight. We are willing to let vindication come from God. 'Do not fret because of evil people,' said the psalmist. 'A little while and the wicked will be no more... But the meek will inherit the land and enjoy great peace' (Ps. 37:1, 10, 11).

Moses lived this way. The final editor of the books of Moses said that Moses himself was more meek than anyone else on the face of the earth (Num. 12:3). When attacked or criticized he would do nothing except fall upon his face before God and pray. Jesus claimed that this was the way he also lived. 'Learn from me, for I am meek...', he said (Matt. 11:29). He deliberately avoided aggressiveness and pride when he rode into Jerusalem 'meek and riding on a donkey' (Matt. 21:5; see Zech. 9:9).

Meekness leads God to specially give us his guidance. 'He guides the meek in what is right' (Psa. 25:9). They get his special protection. 'Yahweh sustains the meek' (Psa. 147:6). They get vindication. The Lord 'crowns the meek' (Psa. 149:4) when he steps in with his final rescue and vindication. When he scatters the nations in judgment, he protects 'the meek and humble who trust in the name of Yahweh' (Zeph. 3:12).[1]

Three things will happen in your life if you live in this way.

1. You will possess the kingdom. More than initial salvation is in mind when Matthew uses this phraseology. 'Possessing the kingdom' means experiencing the powerful blessing of God. *Blessed are the poor in spirit, for theirs is the kingdom of heaven* (5:3). The 'kingdom of heaven' is the reign and rule of our Lord Jesus Christ. It has come already because Jesus came to this world and he is the King of the kingdom. Yet God's reign is coming even more. It is to be 'inherited' day by day in the way in which we live. One day the kingly rule of God will be displayed in a fuller way.[2] But in the here-and-now the

---

1. In these Old Testament references, the Septuagint (Greek Old Testament) uses *praus,* Matthew's word in Matthew 5:5.

2. I have surveyed 'kingdom' in Matthew's Gospel in a simple manner, in my *Enjoying God's Worldwide Church* (Paternoster, originally Sovereign World), ch. 3.

poor in spirit enjoy the blessings of the kingdom of God. God hears their prayers, meets their deepest needs, forgives their sins, writes his requirements upon their hearts. They will shine like stars in the day when God 'purifies' his kingdom, removing all opposition to it, all hypocrisy within it.

It is no accident that 'theirs is the kingdom' is a phrase coming at the beginning and end of the beatitudes (5:3, 10). This is Jesus' main point. The whole 'Sermon on the Mount' is describing what life is like when God rules over us.

2. You will experience divine encouragement. *Blessed are those that mourn, for they shall be comforted* (5:4). God will give them joy and satisfaction and fulfilment. It will begin even in this life.

3. You will inherit the earth. *Blessed are the meek, for they shall inherit the earth* (5:5). The meek 'inherit the earth' even now. All things are theirs because they are Christ's. Everything is worked together to bless them – even the sufferings that come from their enemies. Even in this life God compensates to them the prestige and power which they have lost. They enjoy the presence of God, when their enemies know nothing of it. But there is more to come – the new heavens and new earth in which righteousness dwells.

As I have said, these beatitudes are descriptions more than they are commands, but it is inevitable that we should ask ourselves: how can I enter into these blessings of experiencing God's kingdom, knowing God's encouragement, feeling that he is with me? How can I 'inherit the earth' although I am personally stripped to nothing? As an old song puts it: 'All the fitness he requireth is to feel your need of him.' Trust in the Lord Jesus Christ – again and again – and the blessings of God's rule spring up in your life. The Sermon on the Mount begins with benedictions not maledictions, blessings not curses. As soon as Jesus opens his mouth to speak he is pouring out words of blessing. He does not open his mouth to accuse, to attack, to slander, to criticize – although there was surely plenty to criticize in the disciples. He simply describes the pathway of blessing. It involves not criticizing others, but facing ourselves and casting ourselves on Jesus for mercy.

3. Finding Satisfaction
(Matthew 5:6-8)

Matthew 5:6 follows on very naturally from Matthew 5:3-5. A person who knows he has nothing with which to justify himself before God, and who is grieved at the slowness of the coming of the kingdom of God, and who does not feel that he can defend himself – such a person begins to be hungry for true righteousness in the sight of God.

Blessed are those who hunger and thirst for righteousness, for they shall be satisfied (5:6). Luke's version refers simply to 'hunger' (Luke 6:21), showing us that there is both a personal side and a social side to the sayings of Jesus. Luke's more social emphasis means that the godly

23

are likely to be poor people and they will long for the day when not only they but the world around them conforms to God's will in every area of life. A fully 'righteous' world will have no hunger in it, but we do not have a fully righteous world. The godly long for it to come. But Matthew does not emphasize the social aspect so much.

Jesus refers to actively seeking the righteousness of the kingdom of God. Godliness involves our actively seeking righteousness in every situation. The Christian has to develop a sense of need. It is only when we are hungry that we cry out to the Lord. 'They were hungry ... and their lives ebbed away. Then they cried out to the LORD,' says Psalm 107:5-6. 'Come, all you who are thirsty,' says Isaiah 55:1. Righteousness is a goal; it is something to aim at. Jesus does not congratulate those who are righteous; he congratulates those who want to be and are thirsty for righteousness.

What is it like to be hungry? It tends to distract your attention from anything else you might be doing. A hungry person, whatever else he is doing, tends to be aware that he is hungry! When we 'hunger' for righteousness, it means that whatever else we are doing, this consciousness of God's demand is with us.

It tends to make us push other things aside. A hungry person tends to say to himself, 'Let me get some food, and then I'll do this and that...' A hungry person has a sense of priority. He wants to deal with his hunger first! So with Jesus' 'hunger for righteousness'. It is topmost in our thinking. It is what we are looking for each day.

This 'hunger for righteousness' is a desire that God's righteous will should be done in this world, beginning with me! It is a desire to be right with God, to have a good conscience, to be free from the very desire for sin, to be free from gripping self-centredness and defensiveness, to be like Jesus in the way I relate to other people, and to work out God's will for this world in every area where I can make a contribution.

Blessed are the merciful, for they shall receive mercy (5:7), says Jesus. It is vital to realize that these beatitudes are not 'rules'; they are congratulations. They are like the compliments we receive and the excitement that is generated when we have done well in an exam. 'You passed! Congratulations! Isn't it wonderful? You must be very happy!' This is the atmosphere of the beatitudes. The thought of this beatitude is not, 'This is a rule for your life. You must be merciful!' Of course, such a 'rule' is quite true. We must indeed be merciful! But this is not the atmosphere of the beatitudes. This is not coming to us as a heavy rule. It is coming to us as a congratulation! 'You are in the kingdom!', says Jesus. 'Congratulations! Isn't it wonderful? You must be very happy! You are living in a kingdom of mercy. Isn't it marvellous to live in a kingdom of mercy? Life will be so much more enjoyable.' Jesus is assuming that the disciples are already within reach of living in such a way. They are inside the kingdom already in one sense (although 7:13 will tell them to 'enter' it). They are just at the very doorway of the kingdom; they are standing at the gate. They have already experienced mercy from God. They are about to be people of mercy themselves. 'Congratulations!' says Jesus. 'Blessed are the merciful!'

Martyn Lloyd-Jones pointed out that there is a kind of

correspondence in the beatitudes.[3] The fourth one is like the pinnacle of a mountain. The first three beatitudes are ascending to the pinnacle of the mountain. Only a person who is poor in spirit, and who grieves over his poverty, and who leaves his case with God – is one who truly hungers and thirsts for righteousness. But then such a person begins to experience God's promise: 'they shall be satisfied'. Positive characteristics of the kingdom of God begin to appear in his or her life. Because such a person feels his own weakness, he is merciful to others. He develops an inner purity. He becomes a peace-maker. He 'comes down the other side of the mountain', and mercy, purity, and peaceableness appear in his life. (We shall see how the eighth beatitude fits in later).

Hunger for righteousness

Meekness   Mercy

Mourning   Purity of heart

Poor in spirit   Peace-making

God wants us to be merciful! Mercy is holding back when one feels inclined to punish. Mercy is treating people with leniency and generosity when we feel that they deserve no generosity. Mercy has pity on people's need and on their weaknesses.

The world generally is an unmerciful place full of unmerciful people. But anyone who has experienced the

---

3. D.M. Lloyd-Jones, *Studies in the Sermon on the Mount* (henceforth: *Sermon*; IVP, 1959, 1960; combined volume, Eerdmans, 1971), 1, pp. 106-107 and throughout his early chapters.

kingdom of God is called to be different. As I have said the beatitudes are more descriptions than a list of duties, and yet as they progress the element of 'duty' begins to come in. The Christian maybe cannot create 'poverty of spirit' in his own heart, that takes a miracle of God's grace. We are poor in the things of God, but it takes a miracle of illumination for any of us to see it. The later beatitudes arise out of the earlier beatitudes. If we know our own hearts and own need, it is not so difficult to control ourselves and begin to show mercy to others.

Blessed are the pure in heart, for they shall see God (5:8). This is one of the great themes of Christian holiness: purity of heart. It is what distinguishes pagan morality from true Christian holiness. There are many people who for their own reasons want to live 'good' lives. And there are certainly many people – politicians, pastors and parents especially – who want other people to live good lives. But this 'goodness' that we want in others and in ourselves can often be a very external thing. We are bothered about not disgracing ourselves. We would not like to cause a scandal. It would be nice if people under our care behaved themselves well. All of this is 'morality'. But the Christian faith goes much further than this. It is concerned not simply about 'morality' but about purity of heart. Purity of heart is total honesty and integrity. It is willingness and readiness to have every aspect of one's life become visible in the judgment day, and a lot of it visible now! It is freedom from deceit or pretence, posturing, disguising the way we really are, spiritual camouflage. It is inner commitment to God and to his will.

The three beatitudes that we have considered each end

with a promise or an explanation. 'Blessed are those people,' says Jesus, 'for they shall be satisfied ... they shall receive mercy ... they shall see God' (5:6-8). There are benefits and gains to be got by living the godly life in the power of God's kingly rule. These verses should help us to understand the Bible's way of putting to us the matter of reward. It is not something earthly or material. There is nothing meritorious about them. The rewards God offers us are themselves spiritual. Jesus spoke much about rewards both in this sermon (5:12, 46; 6:1, 2, 5, 16; Luke 6:23, 35) and elsewhere (Matt. 10:41, 42; Mark 9:41). Paul did the same (1 Cor. 3:8, 14; 9:17, 18; 1 Tim. 5:18); so did John (2 John 8; Rev. 22:12). Although Paul insisted that 'justification' does not come by reward (Rom. 4:4), he also insisted that 'good works' do get rewarded. This should show us that justification and reward are different!

There are 'rewards' that come by being in the kingdom of God. And the more we 'work out' our salvation – putting it into practice in the way we actually live – the greater will be our reward. 'They shall be satisfied ... they shall receive mercy ... they shall see God.'

'They shall be satisfied.' God does not tantalize us in the kingdom of God. He gives us promises and then he fulfils them. One of his promises is that he will satisfy our spiritual hunger and thirst. It is a wonderful thing when the day comes in our lives when we realize that God is serious about his promise to satisfy us. Many Christians feel more like orphans than like sons and daughters of God. Many feel as if they are in bondage rather than in liberty. But God has a promise for us. It is part of the kingdom of God.

'They shall be satisfied.' God has many rich promises for us, in this connection. We are crucified with Christ and live by the faithfulness of the Son of God. We become partakers of the divine nature. We may be 'filled' with the Holy Spirit. We may be not only forgiven but also cleansed in conscience. We may be ready to have boldness in the day of judgment – an amazing claim!

What does it mean to be 'satisfied'? It means that there is consciousness that God is giving us major victories, and major progress in the life of godliness. I do not believe the Christian will ever be utterly and totally sinless in this life. There will always be a 'down-drag' upon the Christian – the remains of the sinful nature that stay with us because we are still in an unglorified body – although it should be no more than a petty nuisance! To be 'satisfied' means that we are not hungry any more! We know what Jesus meant when he said 'they shall never thirst again'. To be 'satisfied' means that there is peace between us and God. We are relaxed. We are at ease. We know that we are not perfectly sinless; there is much more that we have to learn. There is still much more growing to take place in our lives. But we are 'walking in the light' and that is enough for God! He will tell us some more about ourselves tomorrow, but for the moment we are living up to what we know – and God is happy with us: we can feel it. This is the spiritual 'reward' that comes to those who hunger and thirst for righteousness.

'They shall receive mercy.' There is a spiritual reward that comes to us when we actually live out our position in the kingdom of God. When we congratulate ourselves for being in a kingdom of mercy, and begin to show mercy to everyone around us, the mercy of God flows back towards us, and we experience it ourselves in deeper measure!

'They shall see God.' The greatest benefit to be got by living the godly life is that we 'see God'. 'Without holiness no person will see the Lord.' It is a mistake to think that this 'seeing God' takes place only at the end of our lives, and is an entirely future reward. Not at all! Sometimes large books get written about the 'summum bonum', the greatest climax of the Christian life.[4] We talk of it as if it is purely future. But no, this 'seeing God' starts straight-away! Consider Hebrews 11:27. Moses made a complete breakaway from his luxurious life in Egypt. He was delivered from fear. He endured the many trials and troubles that came upon him as he served God. What enabled him to do it? 'He endured as seeing him who is invisible.' God might be the invisible God, but Moses could see him! He saw by spiritual awareness Someone whom he could not see with his physical eyes. He became conscious that God was everywhere present with him. Jesus was like that. No one was more conscious of God than Jesus. With the eyes of faith he could see God all the time.

Seeing God starts now! No doubt there will be a great climax to 'seeing God' when we get to heaven (see 1 John 3:2), but like some of the other 'rewards' of being in the kingdom of God, it starts now. It is the greatest blessing that flows from purity of heart.

---

4. Kenneth E. Kirk's *The Vision of God: The Christian Doctrine of the* Summum Bonum (Bampton Lectures for 1928; pub. 1932) is full of thought-provoking information.

4. The Christian's Character
(Matthew 5:9-12)

We have seen that the beatitudes have a climbing-a-mountain structure. Now we are (so to speak) coming down the other side of the mountain. When we reach the climax of the beatitudes (hungering for righteousness), it leads to an outworking in our lives: mercy, purity of heart, a peace-making spirit. So Jesus continues: *Blessed are the peacemakers, for they shall be called the sons of God* (5:9). The idea of being a peace-maker is an active one, not a passive one. It is not that the person passively and 'peacefully' does nothing! The Greek Old Testament text of Proverbs 10:10 actually says 'He that reproves boldly is a peace-maker!' The idea is rather that the person actively goes out of his way to bring reconciliation and harmony. He or she does whatever needs to be done, as much as lies within his powers, to bring reconciliation.

'Peace' is a rather fuller idea in biblical thinking than it is in modern English. The Hebrew idea of 'shalom' is well-known. It includes wholeness and general well-being. Those who have experienced God's 'shalom' become agents of God's 'shalom' in the world. They are recognized as such. 'They shall be called the sons of God.' People will eventually see that they are identified with God's peace-making policy in the world.

'Peace-making' must not be interpreted in a pagan way. Worldly people love the idea of having a 'peaceful' world, a cushy life plus plenty of money to go with it, and our enemies leaving us alone! But this is not at all what the Bible means by peace. When talking of that kind of peace,

Jesus said, 'I have come not to bring peace but a sword!' True peace is reconciliation with God plus all of its side-effects.

The 'peace-maker' is identified with God because God has a peace-making policy in the world. God has already broken down the dividing wall of hostility between Jews and Gentiles, 'so making peace' (Eph. 2:15). More than that, it is God's good pleasure in Jesus 'to reconcile all things to himself, making peace through the blood of his cross' (Col. 1:20). Christians are simply following their Father when they are peace-makers. They are at this point truly 'sons and daughters of God'.

What does it mean in practice to be a 'peace-maker'? We can mention six aspects of the matter.

(i) Concern. The peace-maker is disturbed where he or she finds disharmony or conflict, and wants to do something about it.

(ii) Tact. James says 'The seed whose fruit is righteousness is sown in peace by those who make peace' (Jam. 3:18). It is 'sown' in peace! Some peace-makers are notoriously aggressive in their peace-making! Jesus 'increased in favour with God and man'. Some of us are so concerned to increase in favour with God that we neglect increasing in favour with man. It all comes down to sweetness and tact. No peace-maker can do without it.

(iii) Spirituality. The kind of peace-and-wholeness that Jesus has in mind is gospel-peace. God brings reconciliation 'through the blood of his cross' (Col. 1:20), and in no other way. True spirituality will not try to bring about peace without pointing men and women to the only way of forgiveness and harmony. When Ephesians 2:14

speaks of the dividing wall being broken down between Jews and Gentiles, it was not that gentiles overcame Jews, or Jews overcame Gentiles. It was a matter of both sides coming to reconciliation with God, both being 'brought near by the blood of Christ' (Eph. 2:13).

(iv) Sympathy. The reason why the member of the kingdom of God is able to be at peace is that he alone, she alone, has a true view of life. We understand the world we live in. We are the only ones that do understand it! We know about human sinfulness. We realise that the cause of quarrels is not merely some difficult situation, it is in the people themselves.

(v) Control of the tongue. Enmity and hostility is spread around by the misuse of the tongue. We talk too much, too wildly. We don't know when to stop. 'The tongue ... is set on fire by hell!' The devil's fuelling conflict in the world takes place by our talk, our misuse of the tongue. The peace-maker may actively intervene in troubled situations, but he is a person who knows when to say nothing, when to stop talking.

(vi) Humility. This seventh beatitude follows on from the previous ones. The peace-maker is 'poor in spirit'; he mourns over the delay in perfect peace coming to this world. He is 'meek'. He hungers and thirsts for righteousness. He is 'merciful' and 'pure in heart' and 'sees God' everywhere. It is no wonder he is a peace-maker! Only the King and those in his kingdom of peaceableness can truly be peace-makers.

The eighth of Jesus' beatitudes is an extra comment on the seven. Whereas the first seven beatitudes are complete in themselves as a description of the disciple, the eighth deals not with the disciple himself but with the way in which people react to him. *Blessed are those who are persecuted for the sake of righteousness, for theirs is the kingdom of heaven* (5:10). The words 'theirs is the kingdom of heaven' echoes 5:3 and rounds off the eight beatitudes, showing that the characteristics of the kingdom is their main theme. Verses 11-12 develop the thought: *Blessed are you when people revile you and persecute you and speak evil against you falsely on account of me* (5:11). One notices – what is often missed by pagan admirers of this Sermon on the Mount – how Jesus himself is central in this 'sermon'. It is not 'speaking evil against you falsely' that Jesus mentions; it is 'speaking evil against you falsely on account of me'. The person to be congratulated is the person who is identified with Jesus in ill-treatment. It is not any ill-treatment that is in view; it is ill-treatment coming upon us for the sake of the kingdom of God.

Rejoice and be glad, because in this way they persecuted the prophets who were before you (5:12). It is somewhat surprising that this person who is meek and peaceful, and who hungers for righteousness, should be persecuted. But that is the way it is. One might think that if we really get to live the life of Matthew 5:3-9 people will admire us and approve of us. But it does not work out that way at all! There is something about true spirituality that arouses deep resentment and ghastly ill-treatment from others. Jesus was himself the greatest example. He actually lived the Sermon on the Mount himself. He was poor in spirit, and merciful. He was the greatest peacemaker ever! You would expect Jesus to be admired and praised. You would think that his contemporaries would rush to tell him how wonderful he was. But actually many admired him only because they misunderstood him. When they were actually confronted with his righteousness it made people very angry. He made them feel guilty. A truly godly person tends to make ungodly people feel guilty. When someone is utterly transparent and clean in the way in which he lives, such a person rouses the fiercest opposition in those who are in the grip of sin.

The servant is not greater than his master. Those who live lives approaching that described in Matthew 5:3-9 will rouse animosity in others. The world likes 'nice' people, but there is a difference between being 'nice' and being spiritually-minded. The spiritually-minded are firm, courageous people. They actually do live the life of the Sermon on the Mount – but they arouse great aversion and disfavour as well.

So the Christian may well find himself ill-treated. It might be a matter of words ('when people revile you'). It might be what they say behind your back ('speak evil against you falsely'). It might be worse still. Jesus says, 'Don't worry about it, if it is because of me.' It does have to be because of Jesus! There is no blessing attached to being foolish or awkward or ungraceful. But when you get ill-treated because of your being like Jesus, God is going to bless you.

Persecution is likely to come your way sooner or later. In the world you will have tribulation (see John 16:33). If the world hates you, keep in mind that it hated Jesus first (see John 15:18). Jesus has chosen us out of the world. But if you suffer for Jesus' sake, you need not worry about it. There is a blessing attached to it. Rejoice and be glad!

35

It is not that you are rejoicing in the persecution itself. You rejoice because of the greatness of the reward. In some mysterious way, you are laying up treasure in heaven. God is storing extra blessing for you, just because you have been willing to suffer for the sake of his Son.

'In the same way they persecuted the prophets.' You are following in the footsteps of those who were most used by God. The prophets were the godliest people in Old Testament times. They stood by the word of God and proclaimed it no matter what opposition came to them. If you are like the prophets you will get the honour that comes to the prophets. Before the whole universe Jesus will say to you, 'Well done!'

Don't get depressed or resentful or bitter, if you are ill-treated for Jesus' sake. Don't weep or say, 'How can this be happening to me? Why is God allowing this?' God is watching you. He is putting your tears in a bottle. He is storing it all up in order one day to bless you and reward you, in a way that will make up for every distress. You are in the noble succession of the great men and women of God down the ages.

5. Salt and Light
(Matthew 5:13-16)

The 'sermon' has dealt with the basic description of the disciples of Jesus: what they need (5:3-5), what they desire (5:6), what becomes their positive character (5:7-9), how they are treated (5:10-12). Now in Matthew 5:13-16 Jesus goes on to the way in which they function in the world.

You are the salt of the earth; but if the salt has lost its taste, how shall its saltiness be restored? It is no longer good for anything except to be thrown out and trodden underfoot by men and women (5:13).

Jesus is using two pictures: 'You are the salt of the earth ... the light of the world.' One of these illustrations is negative; the other is positive. Salt purifies; it stops something from going bad. In Jesus' day if you wanted meat to be kept from going bad you rubbed salt in it. Light is more positive; it illuminates and shows the way. Both illustrations show that there is nothing monastic about the Christian life. The references to poverty and meekness do not imply any kind of withdrawal. Far from it! Christians are meant to be involved in society – like light in darkness, like salt amidst putrefaction.

The world has a tendency to decay. Every now and then something happens to make the world optimistic. In the nineteenth century it was reckoned that social problems were about to be eradicated because man was – it was thought – evolving so beautifully that soon war and disease, suffering and crime, were about to be abolished. The First World War of 1914-1918 put an end to talk like that!

Today, people tend to pin their faith to 'democracy'! It is the power of diplomacy that is going to bring such wonderful peace and prosperity for everyone! So it is thought! But Christians know better – if they believe their Bibles. Whatever tinkering may be done by scientists and politicians, the world has a tendency to decay!

Christians tend to prevent decay in the world. Jesus implies that the world has a tendency to go rotten.

37

Christians and they alone have the power to slow down the speed at which the world declines.

How does the church function in this way? It is not just a matter of the clergy taking to politics! That never has in fact made the church to be the salt of the earth; it tends to make the world the putrefaction of the church!

It begins with individuals. Christian people bring a note of joy and peace-making into every place they enter – when they truly are being Christian people. Of course, Christians can slide into spiritual deadness. There is no salt and light then! But when they are rejoicing in God as they should be, they restrain the tendency to sin.

But it is not just a matter of the influence individuals have. The church's work as 'restrainer' of the world's decay is a side effect of the church's evangelism. The first task of the church is to proclaim the gospel, but then the church often finds herself having to act in situations of great distress. You want to share the message of God's grace with some friends, or you go into an area to preach the gospel. You enter a house, a village, a town, a country where you have not been before. But when you get there you find all sorts of other needs as well. You did not go there to meet social needs; you went there to share God's grace. But there is some other need staring you in the face. There is no way you can ignore the need. My wife and I were once seeking to get into an African suburb in Johannesburg (in the old apartheid days). We went there to preach the gospel. But when we got there we found elderly people in such need and distress. We ended up promoting and boosting a kind of 'Relief for the Aged' organisation – it had an unpronounceable vernacular name!

We did not go there to organise relief for the aged; we went there to talk about salvation. But the Christians' influence in the world often arises as a side-effect of their work of preaching the gospel. It is indeed a side-effect – but it is an inevitable side effect. You cannot bump into great need and distress and then do nothing. So – even accidentally – the church ends up being the salt of the earth.

Then when the numbers of Christians are sufficient they start having an even larger impact upon society. Eventually perhaps a society becomes 'Christianized', but then often the so-called Christian society becomes purely a nominal matter. Those who truly know God have to give themselves to the work of evangelism all over again. While the church is being the church, the decay is slowed down.

Salt-less 'salt' is useless. Of course, salt – sodium chloride – cannot become saltless, but in the ancient world it might get mixed with impurities such that no salty taste was left. (It still happens; recently I was in a restaurant in an African city where the 'salt' was definitely not salty!)

When the church ceases to be 'salty' it has become dead and useless. An apostate 'Christian' community rarely recovers. It is despised by God, and despised by men and women. (The thought in Matthew 5:13 deals with something communal; it has nothing to do with personal loss of salvation. The parallels are Romans 11:19-23 and Revelation 2:5, both of which deal with communities.)

When the church ceases to be 'salty' it means that the church has ceased to be the church! If 'salt' without saltiness is not salt, then church without impact upon society has ceased to be 'church'. It is not that the church

39

has to become a political club or a welfare agency. That would only be another way of ceasing to be the church. Christian impact arises out of its central ministry. When we seek to reach out to people we soon discover other needs besides the directly spiritual, and we cannot neglect the other needs. So it all has a restraining effect upon the world putrefaction.

Next, Jesus moves on to a more positive point. The Christian does not only restrain; he or she provides illumination. Each clarifies and enlightens the world. *You are the light of the world*, says Jesus. *A city situated on the top of a hill cannot be hidden* (5:14). *People do not light a lamp and then place it under the grain-measure, but they put it on the lampstand and it gives light to all in the house* (5:15). *In the same way, let your light shine before others so that they may see your good works and give glory to your Father who is in heaven* (5:16).

The world is in darkness, according to the Scriptures. It may have a lot of scientific and technological expertise, but only the Christians have the answer to the spiritual problem that grips the human race. Only the Christians understand that the human problem is vertical; it concerns our relationship to God. Our ultimate plight is not a horizontal matter; there is something more significant than our relationship to other people and to the circumstances we find ourselves in. Only the Christians know the remedy to the human problem. We – and we alone – realize that the darkness of this world is caused by sin and God's anger against it. We – and we alone – appreciate that there is a remedy in the death and resurrection of our Lord Jesus Christ. We know what it means to be 'in Christ'. We know about the outpouring of the Spirit. We have experienced God's Holy Spirit witnessing with our spirits that we are children of God. Only the gospel-message can answer the needs of men and women. I cannot think of anything more challenging and searching than these lines. Are we the salt of the world? Do we have a restraining effect on sin? More importantly: do we illuminate the world and let the men and women of the human race see visibly what is God's intention and purpose for them? I fear that many parts of the Christian church are far from being the 'light of the world', and need God's reviving Holy Spirit. The world is meant to see in us a foretaste of what is on offer for them. We cannot bring down upon ourselves God's fire, but we can brush aside the cobwebs. We can sweep away the ashes, put more fuel on the fire, and plead that God will rekindle righteousness, peace and joy in the Holy Spirit among us again, so that we become 'a city on a hill', God's new Jerusalem.

Jesus said these words first to very 'ordinary' people. 'You,' he said, looking upon a crowd of very ordinary people, 'are the light of the world.' He was speaking to peasants and fishermen and fairly ordinary people of ancient Israel. It was to such people that he said, 'Let your light shine before others...' The Christian faith is a people's movement. It is not just for elite people or scholars or religious officials.

Christians are called to give to the world a visible demonstration of God's scheme for salvation. We begin by realizing that this is our calling. A city situated on the top of a hill cannot be hidden. There is to be no hiding of the fact that we are the people of God. Of course, we avoid triumphalism and pride. We are what we are only because God has had mercy upon us. Once we were blind but now we see – but we did not give ourselves sight.

We are to be bold people. Any kind of timidity is unworthy of what Jesus has done for us. People do not light a lamp and then place it under the grain-measure, and we are not to put ourselves into some position of obscurity out of shyness or timidity. God has not given us a spirit of timidity! We are to 'put our light on a lampstand' – boldly live out what we believe and be fearless amidst those who are watching. When we do that it 'gives light to all in the house'. People see that Christian people are different and they start taking notice.

We take no glory to ourselves and need not bother trying to get attention to ourselves directly. It will come without our trying – so long as we do not hide or run away. We let our light shine before others so that they may see what God has done for us, and what we are willing to do for others. We are not seeking the slightest glory at all. God will give us all the glory we need in his own way and in his own time. We give glory to our Father who is in heaven.

6. Christ in the Scriptures
(Matthew 5:17)

Jesus moves to a new sub-section of his great statement concerning the kingdom. So far he has been giving a description of the disciples and has encouraged them to live out what has happened to them. Now Jesus comes to what must have been a momentous question in the life of his disciples: how does Jesus relate to what God did and said in Old Testament times? And how are they, as Jesus' disciples, to relate to their heritage? The disciples have grown up knowing that Israel should be ruled by the law of Moses. They know about the prophets who preached and wrote messages to Israel, calling Israel back to obedience to the law. How do Jesus and his disciples relate to what has gone before?

Jesus says, *Do not think that I have come to destroy the law or the prophets. I have not come to destroy them but to fulfil them* (5:17).

Matthew 5:17-20 are among some of the most vital texts of Scripture. It is one of the verses which begin 'I have come in order to...'. Jesus liked to say why he came to this world. 'I have come ... to call ...sinners', he would say (Matt. 9:13). Such Scriptures are always of interest because they give us Jesus' own statement of the purpose of his coming.

Jesus, as a good teacher, liked to clear up misunderstandings. Occasionally we find him saying 'Do not think...' (Matt. 10:34) or 'Do you think...?' (Luke 13:2, 4), or 'What do you think?' (Matt. 18:12). Jesus liked to get people to think, and he liked to clear up possible confusion. As the Head of the church, at the right-hand of the Father, he still wants us to think about the Scriptures, and he still wants us to be quite clear as to how he relates to the law and the prophets.

The words 'Do not think' suggest there is danger of misunderstanding. Jesus seemed to be breaking so much tradition. He was certainly hostile to Pharisaism. Was Jesus being so radical that he was bringing a new gospel altogether, without any origins in Israel's history? The answer is: No! 'Do not think that I have come to destroy the law...'

Jesus was making a statement about the entire Scriptures. People often use Matthew 5:17-20 to make the point that God's moral law continues in the gospel. It is certainly true that the gospel does not encourage a lesser morality than that of the Mosaic law. But to get too preoccupied with 'the moral law' misses the point that Jesus is making. People are always interested in morality. Even anti-Christian people talk about how much they like 'morality'. But Jesus is making a statement about the entire Scriptures. He speaks of the law, the prophets, every dot and comma of the entire Old Testament. It includes the Ten Commandments. It includes approximately 2000 verses of legislation in addition to the Ten Commandments. It includes the expositions and developments of the law that are to be found in the remaining thirty-one Old Testament books (Samuel, Kings and Chronicles being counted as three, not six).

'Destroy' normally means 'ruin by pulling down' when referring to buildings. It means 'annul', 'cancel out completely', when applied to legislation. Jesus says 'the law or the prophets', not 'the law and the prophets'. No part of the Scriptures is to be reduced or have its significance brushed aside.

'Fulfil' is clearly the opposite of 'destroy', in this phrase, so it provides clarification of the 'not destroying'. What does 'fulfilling' the Scriptures mean? Let us have some negatives first! It does not mean 'continue' or 'keep going'; this is not the meaning of the word 'fulfil'. It does not mean 'supplement' or 'enlarge' or 'fill out', it does not mean 'expound', it does not mean 'obey'. It does not mean 'cause others to obey'. None of these interpretations gives us the meaning of 'fulfil'. To interpret 'fulfil' aright, our interpretation must meet certain conditions.

(i) The meaning must exist! For example, 'continue as it always was' is not a meaning of 'fulfil'!

(ii) It must have the same meaning both with regard to the law and with regard to the prophets.

(iii) It must cohere with the 'fulfilment' theme of the Gospel of Matthew. We must remember that 'fulfilment' is one of the dominant themes of Matthew's Gospel. Matthew frequently makes the point that various events in the life of Jesus 'fulfil' the Scriptures (see 1:22; 2:15, 17, 23; 4:14; 8:17; 12:17; 13:35; 21:4; 26:54, 56; 27:9, 35). Matthew 5:17 must surely be understood in the same way as the 'fulfilment-quotations' (as they are called) in Matthew's Gospel.

(iv) The meaning must cohere with Matthew 5:21-48. As the Sermon on the Mount unfolds it is clear that Matthew 5:21-48 provides examples of what Jesus has said in Matthew 5:17-20. If, then, we find that at points the details of the law in Matthew 5:21-48 are withdrawn or changed – for example, insistence on giving oaths in the name of Yahweh cancelled and the recommendation made that no oaths be used at all – then this will reflect back on our interpretation of Matthew 5:17, supporting it or refuting it. It will show that 'fulfil' cannot mean 'keep going as it always was'.

(v) Its meaning mainly relates to the life of Jesus. 'I came ... to fulfil.'

(vi) Any view of Matthew 5:17 that wants it to be a statement about only part of the law is obviously wrong. This is why those who like this verse because it asserts (as they see it) the continuity of 'the moral law' are weak in their interpretation. What they say is true – but they do not go far enough. They want to say that 'You shall not commit adultery' is fulfilled and 'Remember the sabbath is fulfilled'. Indeed they are! But this is not saying enough! There are many other aspects of the law and the prophets which are fulfilled also. God demanded that a new nation start which firmly wiped out of existence the vileness of the Canaanites. 'You must utterly destroy them', God said (see Deut. 7:1-5; also Exod. 23:23-24; Deut. 20:16-18). That was 'fulfilled' also – but it does not mean that it simply continues and that Christians have to slaughter their enemies. The law required the existence of a sanctuary like the tabernacle or temple, it required three annual trips to Jerusalem to keep certain festivals. All of this is fulfilled as well. Even tiny parts of the letters in which the Hebrew and Aramaic Old Testament was written will – says Jesus – get 'fulfilled'. To be overly preoccupied with 'the moral law' is to restrict Jesus' main point.

What then does 'fulfil' mean? It refers to the life and ministry of Jesus in which he brings about the events to which the law and the prophets were pointing.

1. *Jesus fulfilled the principles and precepts of the law.* 'The law' begins with the story of Abraham (a point that ought not to be overlooked). Jesus was 'the son of Abraham' (Matt. 1:1) and had the same kind of persistent faith that Abraham had.

Jesus also kept the Mosaic legislation. He literally kept every minute part of the law of Moses. He was circumcised. He went at least three times a year to keep the festivals of Israel. When found guilty by the leading magistrates of Israel, as a sinner on a capital charge, he bore the death-sentence of the law in fulfilment of its requirement against capital sins. Jesus kept the Sabbath every Saturday of his life. He never coveted anyone's possessions. His treatment of 'paying taxes to Caesar' (Matt. 22:15-22) avoided saying anything which would speak against the law about having a Jewish king (Deut. 17:15).

2. *Jesus fulfilled the programmes and prophecies of the Scriptures.* The 'law and the prophets' record God's programme to undo the work of 'the serpent' (Gen. 3:15), to bring about in full measure the ancient prediction that in some way the line of Shem will bring blessing to the people descended from Japheth (Gen. 9:18-27). God has a programme to bring about worldwide blessing through a 'seed of Abraham', the meaning of which gradually becomes clear as God's purpose goes forward. Jesus came in the tribe of Judah to fulfil the promise that God has a king who will bring righteousness to the world. Judah (said the ancient prediction) will be a royal tribe, honoured by all, the 'lion' among the tribes of Israel. 'The sceptre shall not depart from Judah, nor the ruler's staff from between his feet, until Shiloh comes, and the obedience of the nations comes to him'. 'Shiloh' seems to be a name meaning 'the Peaceful One' (see Gen. 49:8-10). The sceptre did not depart from Judah, until after Jesus had come – and then it was totally lost. The Old Testament

47

went on to predict a great Chosen King, a Suffering Servant, an Anointed Conqueror who would come to bring salvation to Israel and thus to the whole world. It is this programme that Jesus was claiming to fulfil.

3. *Jesus fulfilled the patterns and pictures of the scriptures.* The way in which God did things in the times before Jesus revealed God's pattern of salvation. Jesus comes to restore – and more than restore – the prosperity that was given to Adam in Eden. He came to be a 'Moses' announcing God's will from a mountain. He is to be 'the prophet' (Deut. 18:15-19), the fulfilment of all the prophets; 'the priest', the fulfilment of all the priests. He is the fulfilment of the weekly Sabbath, the 'new moons', the seventh year, the year of jubilee, the passover and feast of unleavened bread, pentecost, tabernacles, trumpets, the day of atonement, and the festival of Purim. The passover-and-unleavened bread spoke of redemption by the blood of a lamb, of hasty departure from Egypt and of purity from sin. The Feast of Weeks commemorated the giving of the law (since it was fifty days after passover, just as the events of Sinai took place fifty days after the redemption by the passover lamb). It celebrated fruitfulness and dedication to God. The Feast of Booths, or Tabernacles, spoke of the joy of rich ingathering of God's blessings. Jesus is God's second David, God's priest in the order of Melchizedek. The entire law and prophets were fulfilled by Jesus.

4. *Jesus fulfils the psalms and proverbs.* He is the king of Israel that we meet so often in the Book of Psalms, the One opposed by the kings of the earth, the One who

establishes world-rule in Zion. He is the Wise Man *par excellence*. 'Don't think I have come to brush aside the Bible,' says Jesus, 'for that Bible is entirely about me. I have come to fulfil it.'

7. How Long Does the Law Last? (Matthew 5:18)

Jesus insists that he has no plans to brush aside the Old Testament. On the contrary, he claims that the Old Testament is all about him. He is duty-bound to fulfil it to the letter. He continues: *For truly I say to you, until whatever time the heavens and the earth pass away, not one iota or one part of a letter shall pass away from the law until whatever time all things come to pass* (5:18).

Jesus is explaining what he has already said. He begins with 'For...' There are scholars who ask us to ignore the connecting words in Matthew 5:17-20. We must, they say, take no notice of words like 'For' in verses 18 and 20, and 'therefore' in verse 19. The idea is that these sayings of Jesus were originally separate and have been passed down in the traditions concerning Jesus. Matthew, it is suggested, has weaved them together to make a coherent paragraph. If we want to know the meaning we must look at the verses separately and ignore the connecting links.

But this is surely a strange method to follow. It asks us to ignore the text as we have it (which does have the connecting links) and expound four verses separately without reference to each other. Yet there is no *certain* knowledge that the four verses ever existed separately.

Matthew is telling us the story of Jesus in his own way; and he puts across the gist of Jesus' teaching in his own words. Matthew 5:17-20 might well be a summary of an hour or so of Jesus' teaching in Aramaic. But the version we have before us is Matthew's one: connecting links and all! Actually words like 'for' and 'therefore' are vital clues to the meaning of what Matthew reports. To ignore them would be to throw away vital evidence of his meaning. So Jesus as reported by Matthew says 'For...'. He is explaining what he has already said (in our 5:17).

1. *The Mosaic law has a destiny, a task to fulfil.* Jesus speaks of the law continuing until 'all things *come to pass*' or 'until all things *happen*'. It implies that there are events to take place in fulfilment of the Mosaic law. The law has a programme of action which has to be fulfilled. God is planning to do something and the events that took place on Sinai relate to his plan of action for the world.

Again, there is emphasis on the fact that Jesus is referring to every minutest part of the 'Pentateuch' (the first five books of the Old Testament). There are many aspects to the law. It restrains out of fear of punishment; it includes principles of morality; it demands particular punishments; it includes rituals and ceremonies; it requires the keeping of holy days, and the sacrificial slaughtering of animals. It has regulations about the tribes, about the nation being a unified religion-and-state under threat of death for disloyalty. It has rulings concerning agriculture and economy and even what clothes one is allowed to wear and what food one is allowed to eat. The entire law plays some part in God's plan to bring salvation to the world.

'Is the law against the promises of God?' asked Paul (Gal. 3:21). Certainly not! Every minutest part of the law somehow has a part to play in the history of salvation.

2. *The Mosaic law continues to exercise authority over Israel until every event it predicts has taken place.* It is more stable than the fabric of the universe ('until whatever time the heavens and the earth pass away'*).* No one will ever be able to get rid of it. It has total and utter stability in the purposes of God.

It must be noted however that this authority was always authority over Israel. People often talk as if every nation is to be under the Mosaic law. It is true that in the gospel of Jesus Christ, the outpouring of the Spirit leads to the *fulfilling* of the law among Christian people of every nation and tribe and language and people. But this does not mean that the Sinai law was ever given to the whole world. In fact, the point is often made that the world was *not* given the law. The law itself began by referring to an event that had only been experienced by Israel ('I ... brought *you* out of the land of Egypt ... *You* shall have no other gods before me'). No doubt the commands of the gospel fulfil the law. No doubt all men and women have a conscience (although the Bible does not use the word 'law' in this connection; 'law' refers to Sinai). But there is much more in 'the law' than the 1% or so to be found in the Ten Commandments, and Jesus is explicitly speaking of every letter of the law. It is only Israel who has to have a Jewish king (see Deut. 17:15). It is only the people of Israel who have to keep a Saturday-sabbath under the sanction of the death-penalty. Only Israel is obliged to sacrifice animals every day and travel three times a year to a central sanctuary of the nation. Not one iota, not one part of a letter, will fall aside from the Sinai-law – until it is all fulfilled.

It is sometimes thought that Romans 2:14-15 teaches some kind of 'natural law' other than what was given on Sinai. This would imply that the law has two forms, a 'natural' form, and a 'revealed' form given on Mount Sinai. Nothing like this is ever taught in the Bible. It seems to come from Thomas Aquinas and has in it the atmosphere of Greek philosophy. The law does not have two forms. Romans 2:14-15 is the only passage that can be quoted in this way and certainly must be interpreted differently.[5]

The law of God cannot be brushed aside. It is not eternal, but only its 'fulfilment' can release Israel from it.

3. *The law of God ceases to apply as and when it gets fulfilled.* Until such a time when the law is 'fulfilled' it is enduring and unyielding in its authority. But there is a time when its passing away is envisaged. There are *two* time-clauses is Matthew 5:18: 'until whatever time the heavens and the earth pass away ... until whatever time all things come to pass.' This is unusual. Also it must be noted that Matthew does not use the Greek *heos* ('until'); he uses the Greek *heos an* ('until whensoever') – which implies that the time is open-ended and is dependent on some condition or other being met.

When is the time that the law of God ceases to apply? The two time-clauses give rise to various possibilities of interpretation. Do both time clauses refer to the same time?

---

5. In due course I hope to publish *When God Says 'But'* (Romans 1:1-3:22). Chapters 36-37 deal with the matter more fully.

Or does one clause limit the other time clause? The range of possibilities are many.[6] The first time-clause is the easiest to understand. 'Until whatever time the heavens and the earth pass away' must refer to the end of the age (compare the language of Matthew 24:35; Mark 13:31; Luke 16:17). It implies that the law (in its authority over Israel and in all its minute details) is not eternal, but it is as long-lasting as this age of history.

The more difficult phrase is: 'until whatever time all things come to pass'. Does it refer to the same time? Is it simply repeating the first time-clause? It would seem not. There are reasons to think that 'until whatever time all things come to pass' qualifies and limits the words 'until whatever time the heavens and the earth pass away'. The reasons are:

(i) The double time-reference must have some significance to it, since it is unusual. If both clauses say the same thing it would be unnecessary and repetitive.

(ii) Later in this Gospel we have a similar double time-reference. In Matthew 24 there is a double-reference to the various predictions of the chapter. Of some events it is said: 'This generation will not pass away until all these things take place' (v. 34) – using precisely the same Greek words (*heos an panta tauta genetai*) that we find in Matthew 5:18. The exact wording of Matthew 5:18 is again used of what will happen *in one generation*. In the same chapter – Matthew 24 – there is also reference to the distant end of history. 'But of that day and hour no one knows...' (24:36). Matthew 24:35 and the opening words of Matthew

---

6. See further my *A Theology of Encouragement* (Paternoster, 1995), p.129.

5:18 use similar vocabulary. Matthew 5:18 says the law is long-lasting but not eternal; it lasts as long as this age, and passes away with the end of this age. Matthew 24:35 says that the words of Jesus *are* eternal and will last beyond this age.

(iii) A third reason for thinking that the stability of the law is qualified by what happens in the gospel age is that the instructions of Matthew 5:21-48 do in fact modify the precise requirements of the law – as we shall see. At the end of the Gospel (Matt. 28:20) the final authority is not the Mosaic law at all, but the words of the risen Jesus: 'teaching them to observe all that I – the risen Lord Jesus Christ – have commanded you'. This suggests that the precise requirements of the law have been left aside and Jesus' instructions remain as the final authority for the Christian. For those who heed the salvation in Jesus, the law in its precise 13th century BC format does *not* remain in place until the end of the age.

The conclusion must be that where the authority of Jesus is accepted. Jesus, not the Mosaic law, is the final authority and it is his commands that we heed and obey. 'All things' predicted by the law must be the death and resurrection of Jesus, the removal of the kingdom from the leaders of Israel, and the fall of Jerusalem. The law is fulfilled by Jesus. The penalties of the law fall on him. For those who will not receive him, the penalties for breaking the Sinai covenant fall on Israel and Jerusalem is to be destroyed.

4. *One day the Mosaic law will cease for ever.* There is a dual end-time for the law. For those who receive Jesus, authority is transferred from the law to Jesus. For those

people of Israel who will not receive Jesus, the judgments of the law stand and will soon be brought to pass. The authority over the Christian will not exactly be the Mosaic law; it will be the requirements of Jesus which 'fulfil' the law. One day 'the law' will cease for everyone. For the Christian life 'under the law' has ceased already; it has been 'fulfilled' by Jesus. Yet the new life under the risen Lord Jesus Christ is not *less* godly than life under the law. Life under Jesus Christ fulfils everything that the law was pointing to. The Christian does not disrespect the Mosaic law but nor is he 'under' it in a simple unsophisticated manner. He 'fulfils' it (as Matthew would say) by hearing the commands of the risen Lord Jesus Christ or (as Paul would say) by walking in the Spirit.

8. Greatness in God's Kingdom (Matthew 5:18-19)

Jesus' words in Matthew 5:18 are one of the strongest statements of the verbal inspiration of the Old Testament. The scriptures in their original languages and in the original documents written by the biblical writers are utterly trustworthy. Jesus himself affirmed the divine reliability of every letter of the Pentateuch, even of every part of a letter. The scriptures are utterly true in everything they assert, and in everything they deny. In doctrine they have no error. In each stage of history they set forth God's will for the life of his people at that time with total faithfulness. When they touch upon matters of science or geography they continue to be trustworthy in everything they affirm. Translations may be defective and copyists of manuscripts

55

may make mistakes, but the writings of the men of God who produced the Old Testament scriptures are 'God-breathed' – and we have no reason to think the New Testament is any different.

It is one's attitude to this unique sanctity of the entire scriptures that affects whether a man or woman is truly great in experiencing the royal power of God. Our attitude to the written 'Torah' (Genesis–Deuteronomy) is a case in point. In Matthew 5:19 Jesus moves from his own attitude to the Mosaic law to that of his disciples and followers. *Whoever therefore shall relax one of these least commandments, and shall teach men and women in that manner, such a person shall be called the least in the kingdom of heaven. But whoever shall obey them and teach them, such a person shall be called great in the kingdom of heaven* (5:19).

There is a connection between Jesus' attitude to the law and that of his disciples: 'Whoever *therefore*' – in the light of the purpose of Jesus' coming – 'shall break one of these...' If Jesus upholds the Mosaic law, fulfilling it in his own life and ministry and in his death, then Jesus' disciples may be expected to fulfil the law also. The disciples will follow the pattern set by Jesus himself.

1. *There is variation of greatness in the kingdom of God.* It is often assumed that everyone is equal in the kingdom of God. Matthew 20:1-16 is often pressed to make this point (although to get an *exceptional and unparalleled* point of teaching from one parable is surely a mistake, and the point of the parable is more to speak of God's sovereign rights than to insist on total equality in the

kingdom). The Reformation doctrine of 'justification by faith only' (which is truly biblical) is sometimes extended as if it meant that there are no differences among disciples at all. But this is a slip in doctrine. There is equality of all in needing a Saviour, and there is the equality of every believer in God's providing new birth and justification and sonship for all equally. But this does not mean that all Christians are equally pleasing to God. There are dozens of scriptures that teach the opposite. A Christian must live to please God, and pleasing God is not automatic. Some Christians please God more than others. Some sow to the Spirit and reap eternal life back from the Spirit. Some have treasure in heaven more than others. So Jesus is not saying anything very unusual in speaking of greatness and smallness in the kingdom. There are some who are first and others who are last in the kingdom of God. *Disciples* are asked to press into the kingdom.

Variation of greatness in the kingdom of God extends even beyond the grave. In the judgment day of Christ some 'suffer loss' and are saved 'through fire'. Others receive a reward (1 Cor. 3:11-15).

2. *Greatness and smallness in the kingdom is determined by one's attitude to the law of God.* In one's personal life ('Whoever ... shall relax ... whoever shall obey') and in one's teaching ministry ('Whoever ... shall teach ... whoever shall ... teach...'), our attitude to the scriptures brings smallness or greatness, disgrace or honour, in the kingdom of God.

There are some questions to be asked here since Jesus himself seems to 'relax' particular requirements of the

Torah (as the Pentateuch is called in Hebrew) and he seems
to teach others to do so also. Matthew 5:19-20 are among
the many sayings of Jesus that could not have been well
understood until after the Day of Pentecost. When they
were originally spoken, the disciples must have been
puzzled about what they meant. How could Jesus speak
of not relaxing the law and yet himself seem to bring some
changes in what 'obedience' means in the kingdom of
God? How could there be a greater loyalty to the written
Scriptures than that shown by the scribes and Pharisees?
The disciples must have been baffled and perplexed until
the experience of the Spirit brought more light.

These phrases have been interpreted in various ways.
For some expositors, the disciples are expected simply to
continue the Mosaic requirements in the same manner as
when they were given in the days of Sinai. Nothing must
be relaxed! Robert Banks sidesteps this by taking 'these
commandments' to refer not to the commands of the law
but to the commands that Jesus is *about* to give in Matthew
5:21-48.[7] In his view 'These commands' looks forward to
what Jesus is just about to say. This would certainly be
easier to understand but it does not seem a natural way of
taking Jesus' words.

For others – and I believe they are right – there is a
'dispensational' element in these words. I am not arguing
for the system of theology known as 'Dispensationalism';
but there are clearly *some* matters in the days of Jesus
which were 'dispensational' and are no longer appropriate
to the Christian. Matthew 5:23 refers to disciples offering

---

7. See R. Banks, *Jesus and the Law in the Synoptic Tradition* (CUP,
1975), p.223.

the burnt offering in the temple and tells them how to do it. Surely a Christian must take that in a 'dispensational' manner. Just as Jesus literally kept the Mosaic law, but prepared the way for something entirely higher, so he wished the disciples to do the same. Jesus' disciples kept the sabbath, every Saturday. They would have tithed and ate only meat from which the blood had been drained. They kept the passover festivals as Jesus kept the passover festivals. During his lifetime the law was upheld by Jesus literally and in strict accord with the letter of the law. The disciples were taught to do the same – for the moment. All 2000 verses of legislation in 'the Torah' were to be obeyed – for the moment.

Yet Jesus clearly is moving in a direction in which the Mosaic law will be transcended, not by being disregarded but by being outclassed. Jesus will in this very sermon be giving his own commands which will outstrip and outclass the equivalent commands in the Mosaic law.

(i) He will forbid anger – and so introduce a requirement which puts the sixth commandment in the shade.

(ii) He will forbid adultery in its earliest beginnings, whereas the law only demanded punishment when the act of adultery had been committed.

(iii) Jesus will speak against divorce almost entirely – and so cancel a proviso allowed in the law.

(iv) Jesus generally speaking forbids the taking of oaths, although the law actually demanded them.

(v) Jesus forbids revenge as part of personal relationships, although the law did no more than restrain revenge from becoming too extreme.

(vi) Jesus forbade any kind of hate towards an enemy

59

but the law allowed the slaughter of the Canaanites and sometimes demanded animosity towards certain kinds of enemies.

These commands of Jesus are not 'expositions' of the law. They are Jesus' *own* commands. Yet none of them exactly work against the godliness of the law. Even a command which contradicts the law does so by moving in the direction of *greater* godliness. So it does not work against the *intent* of the law. The law took Israel in the direction of godliness. Sometimes it so took into account the hardness of the human heart that it was only a *small* step in the direction of holiness. Think how small a step in the direction of godliness was to be found in the law concerning divorce. Jesus went much further in the direction of righteousness in his equivalent instruction in the same area of concern.

So when Jesus speaks of anyone who breaks 'one of these least commandments', he must refer partly to *literally* keeping them in that pre-Pentecostal stage of history. But he must also expect the disciples to be outstripping the law and moving on to a righteousness which was greater than anything the law envisaged. In so doing they would not be 'relaxing' the requirements of obedience. They would be expecting more, not less, in the life of godliness; higher spirituality not lower levels of obedience. Unless they did strive for such higher-than-the-law righteousness they would have small experience of the kingdom. Unless they took seriously the law – and even outstripped it – they would eventually face dishonour and disgrace within the kingdom of God.

3. *Reward in the kingdom is largely a matter of honour or disgrace.* Depending on their attitude to the demands of the Scripture, fulfilled and then upgraded by Jesus, the disciples would be 'called the least' or 'called great' in the kingdom of heaven. The important word is 'called'. Part of the reward of faithfulness in the kingdom is one's eventual reputation. Jesus was, for his obedience, given a name above every name. He was called 'Lord' in a greater way than ever. Abraham's inheritance included the promise, 'I shall make your name great.' Our reputation, our name, what we are 'called' – will be part of our eternal reward. Maybe we shall never be 'called' anything great in this world, but sooner or later honour will come to those who heed the voice of Jesus, upgrading the demand of the law into his own demand for the godly life.

9. Surpassing Righteousness
(Matthew 5:20)

Jesus continues to explain that he requires the highest imaginable standard of righteousness. No details are yet spelled out. Soon Jesus will go on to speak of freedom from anger, sexual purity, commitment in marriage, simplicity in speech, passivity amidst insult and – the climax of his six points – love towards a neighbour. His 'surpassing righteousness' will be expounded, but for the moment, Jesus is still speaking of principles.

For I say to you unless your righteousness shall exceed the righteousness of the scribes and the Pharisees you shall not at all enter into the kingdom of heaven (5:20).

The scribes and Pharisees are mentioned because they are the people who, more than any other, will be concerned to know whether Jesus is brushing aside the Mosaic law. Jesus says he is not ignoring the claims of righteousness and of obedience to the Scripture. Nor will his disciples do so. But the precise way in which he and his people relate to the Mosaic law is distinctive. It is not simply a matter of continuing under it in the old way. Nor is it a matter of Jesus and his disciples simply becoming like the Pharisees. The righteousness that Jesus brings into being will be altogether greater, altogether higher.

Three questions call for our attention: (i) What is the righteousness of the scribes and Pharisees? (ii) What is the righteousness that exceeds it? (iii) What does it mean to enter the kingdom of heaven?

1. Consider the third question first. *What does it mean to enter the kingdom of heaven?* It is a mistake to think that Jesus is simply referring to the disciples first 'conversion', or their first experience of coming to faith. It is true that occasionally (but rarely) 'enter the kingdom' seems to refer to one's first experience of salvation. That seems to be the meaning in John 3:3 and 5. But more often, 'entering the kingdom' is more than that. These disciples have come to their first faith already! They are already the light of the world and the salt of the earth. At this particular stage of ministry Jesus is taking his more advanced followers away for special teaching. On this same occasion he will appoint twelve of them to be apostles. He is not conducting an evangelistic crusade. Rather he is giving teaching for those who are already deeply committed to him. So Matthew

5:20 is not an evangelistic text. Nor is it right to think that the 'righteousness' that is superior to the scribes and the Pharisees is the 'imputed righteousness of Christ'. That is what it would mean if Paul were talking! But Jesus is not dealing with any kind of 'imputed righteousness' here. He is speaking of our actual life, the way we live. There is an actual righteousness which far outstrips that of the scribes and Pharisees . If we live in the way Jesus wants we shall *experience* the kingdom of God. 'Entering the kingdom' does not mean 'coming to first salvation'. It means laying hold of the righteousness, peace and joy that is to be experienced by the people of God.

2. Our second question, then, must be: *what was the righteousness of the scribes and Pharisees?*[8] They were a people who were intensely loyal to the smallest details of 'the Torah', although they spoke more of Moses than they did of Abraham, more of law than of faith. Yet their righteousness was largely an external righteousness. It was a 'righteousness' that was devoid of compassion and worried more about reputation than about reality. The scribes and Pharisees could be grossly inconsistent. Jesus would call them 'whitewashed tombs' (Matt. 23:27) and urge them to cleanse the inside of their lives (23:26). The 'righteousness of the scribes and Pharisees' was intensely loyal to the scriptures and yet had no inner purity and compassion. Despite all of their love of the law, they had no experience of the kingdom of God in their lives.

---

8. I have surveyed the relevant texts in Matthew that speak of scribes and Pharisees in my *Encouragement*, pp.131-133.

3. Our last question brings us to the heart of Jesus' words: *what then does it mean to 'exceed the righteousness of the scribes and the Pharisees'*? There are at least four major ways in which Jesus commends a greater righteousness.

It involves purity of heart. With all of their concern for uprightness and a good reputation, the scribes and Pharisees were not very bothered about internal purity – but the disciple knows that it is 'the pure in heart' who see God. Even the Mosaic law did not say much about the heart. In the original legislation[9] the word 'heart' was never used. Only forty years later did Moses say things like 'O that their hearts would be inclined to fear me'. Within forty years of the giving of the law it was clear that it was not changing anyone's heart. But the 'righteousness that exceeds that of the scribes and Pharisees' includes the heart!

It is related to Jesus rather than to the Torah. Jesus asks his people to focus on himself. He says 'I say unto you'. In these words the law is not mentioned! The entire Sermon on the Mount draws attention to Jesus himself. He says, 'I came to fulfil the law ... I say to you'. Earlier he has spoken of suffering for his sake (5:11) – not suffering for the sake of the law. He repeatedly says 'I say', not only in the six contrasts of 5:21-48, but also further on in the Sermon (6:2, 5, 25, 29). He will speak of the wisdom of heeding his own words (7:24) – not the words of the Mosaic law. In the final judgment the lost will be told, 'I never knew you' (7:23). Their 'lawlessness' was not so much transgression of Moses' commands; it was transgression of the words of Jesus. Their house was

9. I have listed the approximately 1500 verses in my *Living Under Grace* (Nelson Word, 1994, distributed by Paternoster), pp.175.

built on sand because they did not heed *Jesus'* words. When Jesus gives his last words on earth, he will speak of 'teaching them to observe all that I commanded you' and promises to be with the disciples for ever. We may contrast this with (for example) Joshua 1:7: 'Be careful to do according to the law which Moses my servant commanded you...' The commissioning of Old Covenant days after the death of Moses mentions the law; the commission of Jesus after his own death mentions himself! Jesus is the new passover lamb; Jesus is the law. And fifty days after passover will not come a new Mount Sinai – but the outpouring of the Spirit. From then on the law will be fulfilled through the commands of the risen Jesus and 'the law of the Spirit of life in Christ Jesus' (Rom. 8:2).

This 'exceeding righteousness' focuses on love and compassion. Much of the remainder of the Sermon on the Mount will develop this point. It will come in at the end of the six contrasts (5:43-48), and be mentioned in the Lord's prayer (6:12, 14-15). It will be the single point which summarises the law and the prophets (7:12).

This 'exceeding righteousness' is ready to follow the hints of the law and yet progress beyond it. There is nothing wrong with the law. When people want to go beyond the law it often seems that they are criticizing it. The apostle Paul had this problem. 'Is the law sin?' he would ask. He was so eager to go *beyond* the law that he seemed to be accusing it of being sinful. But his answer is: 'May it never be! On the contrary...!' 'The law is holy ... righteous...good' (Rom. 7:7, 12). Jesus faced this very problem. 'Do not think that I have come to destroy the law...' (5:17). If someone says 'I am not under the law', he or she is taken to mean 'I am not under any requirement of righteousness' – which is not what they mean at all! The law was a step in the direction of holiness. It took into account the hardness of heart that was to be found in Israel in the thirteenth century BC (or at whatever date the events of Sinai are given). It was a 'shadow' of what God was about to do in the history of the world in bringing a Saviour who would be a King of Righteousness. The law fore-shadowed what God would do. Even the moral law was only a 'shadow' of the righteousness of heart which Jesus would bring.

Anyone living under Jesus will 'fulfil' the law. The key word is 'fulfil' What the law could not do Jesus has done (see Rom. 8:3)! We are released from the law in order that the requirement of the law might be *fulfilled!* How? In what people? *In those who do not walk according to the flesh but according to the Spirit.* By being free from the law we fulfil the law – by walking in the Spirit or (as Jesus himself would say) by keeping everything commanded us by the risen Lord Jesus Christ.

The 'righteousness that exceeds that of the scribes and Pharisees' looks at the law and sees a *shadow* there. It then looks at Jesus and hears his voice and his commands. His commands concern the heart; generally those of the law do *not*. Only the tenth commandment and the demand for love (mentioned in the law in Leviticus 19:18 amidst some very obscure legislation, but picked out by Jesus as part of the twofold 'great commandment') involve the heart. When Moses said, 'O that their hearts would be inclined to fear me' (Deut. 5:9), he was saying something not in the law itself given forty years earlier.[10]

Living under Jesus is largely a matter of focusing on

love. 'Let us once and for all get rid of the idea that our Lord came to set up a new law; or to announce a code of ethics', said Dr. Martyn Lloyd-Jones.[11] We *do* fulfil the law, but we exceed it by focusing on Jesus and hearing his commands of love. Not any old 'love'! But the kind of 'love' required by Jesus, a love that fulfils the law and even outstrips it, a love that does not steal or commit adultery, a love that keeps its talk simple and pure. In such a way we outstrip the law and we start experiencing the kingdom of God. God blesses us. He hears our prayers. We feel his touch of power working within us. We become a channel of blessing to others. Unless we actually do live this way we shall never be experiencing the kingdom of God flowing in power in our lives.

10. Anger
(Matthew 5:21-26)

Jesus begins to give examples of what he has said in Matthew 5:17-20. There are six paragraphs dealing with anger (5:21-26), adultery (5:27-30), divorce (5:31-32), oaths (5:33-37), revenge (5:38-42) and love (5:43-48). In each case Jesus shows how his requirement 'fulfils' the law – although it is never identical to it.

First, Jesus deals with anger:

You have heard that it was said to the people of long ago, 'You shall not kill', and whoever kills shall be liable to

---

10. See M.A. Eaton, *Living Under Grace*, (Nelson Word), 1994, Chapter 41 for further details.

11. See Lloyd-Jones, *Sermon*, 1, p.214.

judgement (5:21). But I say to you: everyone who is angry with his brother shall be liable to judgement, and whoever says to his brother, 'You worthless imbecile' shall be liable to the council; and whoever says 'You fool!' shall be liable to the fiery Gehenna (5:22). Therefore if you are bringing your gift to the altar and there you remember that your brother has some complaint about you (5:23), leave your gift there before the altar and first go and be reconciled to your brother, and then come and offer your gift (5:24). Quickly become well disposed to your opponent while you are with him on the way, lest your accuser hand you over to the judge, and the judge to the attendant, and you are put into prison (5:25). Truly I say to you, you will never get out from there until you repay the last coin (5:26).

Bitterness and anger! Hatred and animosity! Think about it. What causes such bitterness of spirit? Sometimes it is frustration. It is infuriating when things are not going the way we want them to go, and others are the cause of the blockage. King Ahasuerus was angry with his wife because she would not do as he wished (Est. 1:12). Balaam was angry even with his donkey because he could not get the donkey to do what he wanted. Sometimes anger arises from a sense of injustice. When we see something that is unjust – especially if it is oneself that is the object of the injustice – it rouses anger. David was angry about the story Nathan told him (2 Sam. 12:5) – until he realised it was about himself. Sometimes anger is a side effect of jealousy. Cain was angry with Abel because Abel's sacrifice was acceptable to God but his own was not (Gen. 4:5-6). Saul was angry with David because David was more successful than Saul (1 Sam. 18:8).

Not all anger is wrong. Nehemiah was angry when he discovered the poor were being badly treated (Neh. 5:6). Jesus was angry when he found his Father's temple being misused (Matt. 21:12-13). Sometimes people are thought to be angry when they are firm and clear about some matter of principle. Paul was not guilty of bitterness when he wrote Galatians 1:8-9. John was not angry when he wrote 2 John 9-11. But people cannot always distinguish between firm principles and anger! Jesus was not bitter when he called the Pharisees 'whitewashed sepulchres' or 'hypocrites' (Matt. 23:15) or 'blind fools' (Matt. 23:17) – the very word used in Matthew 5:22. But the kind of anger mentioned by Jesus is clearly abusive, vindictive anger. As always in the Sermon on the Mount, Jesus is dealing more with our attitudes than he is making hard-and-fast rules. He himself could call someone a fool when necessary, but he never had any love of abusive, insulting talk, used as a way of expressing animosity of heart.

How does anger show itself? Jesus tells us. In insulting language: 'You worthless imbecile! You fool!' In violence (Saul threw a spear at David; the high-priest of Matthew 26:65 tore his clothes in rage). In punishment (when Pharaoh was angry with his butler and baker, they were imprisoned – Gen. 40:2). With sullenness ('Ahab was sullen and angry' – 1 Kgs. 20:43). Righteous anger also shows itself. Of course, people might express themselves forcefully without it being bitterness of spirit. People in Bible times might 'tear their clothes' in distress, as Job's comforters did (Job 2:12). Jesus made a whip and drove out the sellers in the temple. Moses smashed the first copy of the ten commandments.

What does the Mosaic law say about anger? The answer might be surprising to some people: nothing! It only restrained the expression of anger in murder. There was plenty of anger around in the days of early Israel. Esau was angry with Jacob (Gen. 27:45). Jacob got angry with his wife (Gen. 30:2). Moses was at one stage 'hot with anger' against Pharaoh (Exod. 11:8) and at another time angry with the idolatry of Israel (Exod. 32:19). Yet there was no legislation against anger. The law mentions the danger of *God's* becoming angry but it never has anything to say about anger among the Israelites.

If we understand the Mosaic law, we shall not find this so surprising. And if you are surprised by it, you have yet to understand the genius of the Mosaic law! The Mosaic law was mainly concerned with external behaviour. It was administered by magistrates and councils of elders and heads of families. It did not have much to say about the heart. It did not legislate against anger – unless and until that anger showed itself in some visible and external crime. What the law spoke against was not the attitude of the heart. A civil code cannot deal with the heart very much. But the law legislated against that anger showing itself in murder.

Take the case of Simeon and Levi who were so angry that they killed the villagers of Shechem (Gen. 34:25, 26). Genesis 49:6, 7 says: 'they have killed men in their anger ... Cursed be their anger, so fierce, and their fury, so cruel.' If Simeon and Levi had been judged by the (later) Mosaic law they should have been executed. But they would not have been executed for their anger; they would have been executed for their murder. The law – except for the tenth commandment – did not judge the heart. It judged only the deed. It was only the tenth commandment which went deeper than the general run of the Mosaic law.[12]

How does Jesus handle the matter? Although Jesus refers to the sixth commandment, Jesus is not *expounding* the sixth commandment. He is rather taking the same area of behaviour (the sanctity of life) and giving his requirement which is much higher than the Mosaic law.

It is sometimes said that Jesus is contrasting his teaching not with the law but with the *misuse* of the law in the first century. We shall consider this matter as we go along, but it can be said now that the wording of Matthew 5:21, 27, 31, 33, 38 and 43 in every case fairly represents the Old Testament requirement. Also the change of tense must be noted. It is not: 'It *is* said ... but I say to you'. Rather the wording is: 'It *was* said ... but I say to you'. Also Jesus does not say: 'You have heard that it was said ... but Moses *truly* says ...'. It would have been quite easy to say something along these lines. But what Jesus actually says is: 'You have heard that it was said ... But I say to you...'. There is no special significance in the fact that 'said' is used rather than 'written' ; 'said' is also used in Romans 9:12 and Galatians 3:16 where the reference is to the voice of God as recorded in Scripture. The words of Exodus 20:13 were in fact *spoken* by God before they were written down, and the people were in front of Mount Sinai hearing them. The first half of the contrast ('You have heard that it was said ...') refers to the Mosaic law. The words 'Do not murder' exactly reproduce the wording of Exodus

12. On this point, see my exposition of Romans 7:7-12 in *Living Under Grace* (Paternoster), and my *Applying God's Law* (forthcoming, Paternoster), chs. 26-27.

20:13 – the sixth commandment. 'Liable to judgment' is a fair summary of the Old Testament legislation in Exodus 21:12, Numbers 35:12 and Deuteronomy 17:8-13. The second half of the contrast does not mention the Mosaic law at all!

How then does Jesus warn us away from anger?

(i) He deals with the attitude and words more than with crimes that could be handled by magistrates.

(ii) He pays special attention to the community of disciples (referring to 'your brother'). There must be total forgiveness of all fellow-disciples if our prayers and our worship are to be acceptable.

(iii) He warns us that sin has spiritual judgments. The law spoke of earthly judgments. Jesus speaks of *God's* 'council' and of 'Gehenna'. The law dealt with visible earthly crimes and administered visible earthly judgment, but Jesus refers to spiritual attitudes and judgment which extend beyond the grave (a point also made by Hebrews 12:25).

So (iv) Jesus urges urgent action to correct soured relationships – putting reconciliation with a brother or sister above worship at the temple (a point of Jesus' teaching that was relevant before but not after AD 70), and

(v) warns that even his disciples will have a taste of Gehenna if action is not taken to curb anger.

If it is asked: how can Jesus warn disciples against 'Gehenna', it may be replied that the text does not go into such a question and one's answer will reflect one's overall theology.

(i) For some, the answer will be: disciples can lose their salvation.

(ii) For others, the answer will be: some so-called disciples will turn out not to have been disciples after all.

(iii) For yet others, the answer is: salvation is secure but Scripture warns of 'salvation through fire' and uses the word 'Gehenna' in this connection.

Answer number (i) is, I believe, mistaken. A combination of (ii) and (iii) is the answer required by the general teaching of Scripture – as I see the matter.

The Christian is not under the Mosaic law; he or she has something altogether greater as his 'rule of life' – the personal instruction of Jesus, which 'fulfils' the law but goes beyond it. 'Get rid of anger' said Paul (Eph. 4:31; Col. 3:8). 'Be slow to anger' said James (Jas. 1:19). Outbursts of anger are deeds of the flesh, said Paul (Gal. 5:20). They were all following their Master. Everyone who is angry with his brother will be liable to judgment.

11. Sexual Purity
(Matthew 5:27-30)

Next, Jesus has something to say about sexual purity.

1. First Jesus recalls the Mosaic law. The seventh of the Ten Commandments (see Exodus 20:14 and Deuteronomy 5:18) forbade a sexual relationship between a man and a married woman within the community of Israel. Jesus quotes it. *You have heard that it was said, 'You shall not commit adultery* (5:27). It did not originally refer to everything that a modern Christian considers to be immorality. In ancient Israel, marriages with foreign women were forbidden altogether (see Deut. 7:3-4).

'Adultery' had to do with the women married to Israelite men. Both the man and the woman who committed such a crime were, under Mosaic law, to be executed by their being stoned to death (Lev. 20:10; Deut. 22:22, 24). The law treated a betrothed woman as a married woman for the purpose of this ruling (Deut. 22:24). A sexual relationship with a single girl was a different crime (see Deut. 22:28). Polygamy, the having of more than one wife, was not against the Mosaic law. Nor was concubinage, having a female slave who was sexually available but was not fully a wife.

Much of this might surprise and horrify a Christian, but this is itself a reminder that the Mosaic law was considerably inferior to life in the Holy Spirit.

2. Next, Jesus puts his own requirement. As always Jesus goes much higher than the law. The law condemned only the external deed. Jesus says: *...but I say to you that everyone who looks at a woman with the purpose of getting her to lust has already committed adultery with her* (5:28). His teaching is deeper and wider altogether than that of the law. He is concerned about *any* woman single or married, Jew or Gentile – unlike the seventh commandment which was only designed to protect a married Israelite woman. He is concerned about the earliest stages of the sin in the signalling of the eyes. The law did not apply in ancient Israel until the deed was done. Jesus starts further back in the intents of the heart.

The translation should probably be 'with the purpose of getting her to lust.'[13] It is not referring to 'lusting in the heart' but to the earliest attempt of a man to arouse a woman's interest in his planned immorality. Some languages have a special word for making a signal with the eyes in order to suggest sexual availability! Jesus is not dealing with fleeting imaginations. Certainly he is not saying temptation is itself sin. Rather he deals with the earliest intention or purpose. Even if the woman says 'No' to such a 'signal with the eyes', a sin has been committed. But an unfulfilled intention was not touched by the Mosaic law.

3. Thirdly, Jesus gives a word of instruction about handling the matter of sexual purity. The responsibility for our purity rests on us. Jesus is telling *us* to do something. There was once teaching that was popular among Bible-believing Christians to the effect that the Christian purity proceeds as we 'let go and let God'. It is not so common nowadays, but we still need a reminder. We have to take part in our own sanctification. In this matter of purity, prayer alone will not be enough. God purifies us by rousing us to the point where we purify ourselves!

> But if your right eye causes you to stumble, pluck it out and throw it away from you. For it is better for you that one part of your body perish than that your whole body be thrown into Gehenna (5:29). And if your right hand causes you to stumble, cut it off and throw it away from you. For it is better for you that one part of your body perish than that your whole body depart into Gehenna (5:30).

---

13. It is likely that *auten* is the subject of the infinitive; the object of the verb found here generally takes the genitive. See further K.Haacker, Der Rechtsatz Jesu zum Thema Ehebruch (Mt 5,28), *Biblische Zeitschrift*, 21 (1977), pp.113-116.

There is suffering in this self-purification. Jesus says we might have to 'pluck out' something that is very precious to us, something we feel we need. We pluck out a right eye; we cut off a right hand. The language is not literal, but it gets across the idea of taking out of our life something that is very precious.

Jesus recognizes that people vary and that one thing might specially tempt one person and another thing specially tempt another. '*If* your right eye causes you to stumble, pluck *that* out ... but (on the other hand) *if* your right hand causes you to stumble, cut *that* off and throw it away ...' His words are accepting that some might be tempted in one area more than others are. And we might be specially vulnerable to temptation in one section of our life but less so in another section of our life.

The implication is that we should get to know ourselves and recognize our own weaknesses. If sexual temptation is a particular problem – as it is for many people – we are to take appropriate action. It might well involve suffering, but we face the suffering involved and accept it. The same principles apply in other matters (proneness to alcoholism, inclination to bitterness or bad temper, inclination to cowardice or fearfulness). We all have our own vulnerabilities.

Some of Jesus' hearers were on this same occasion about to be appointed apostles. Quite mature disciples have to pay attention to these matters. 'The flesh' – the fallen sinful nature – 'produces desires against the Spirit'. It will always be true until we get to heaven.

This matter affects our eternal reward in heaven. I have already suggested that our interpretation of 'Gehenna' in the Sermon on the Mount will reflect our overall theology. Salvation is secure, but Scripture warns of 'salvation through fire' and uses the word 'Gehenna' in this connection.[14] Jesus spoke of the anger of God against disciples who neglected to work out their salvation (Matt. 5:22, 25-26, 29; 7:13, 14, 19, 23, 27). The Greek word is used twelve times (Matt. 5:22, 29, 30; 10:28; 18:9; 23:15, 33; Mark 9:43, 45, 47; Luke 12:5 and Jas. 3:6) and always denotes punishment. It comes for the first time in the Sermon on the Mount on the lips of Jesus (Matt. 5:22, 29, 30), when it is used in warnings given to disciples. Disciples are warned of liability to 'the hell of fire' (Matt. 5:22) and a prison from which there is no escape until the last coin is restored (Matt. 5:26; note also Luke 12:57-59). These warnings say that the whole body may go into Gehenna, a reference to resurrection. Matthew 7:13 also warns against 'destruction'. Matthew 7:26-27 refers to the foolish person whose house collapses in a time of storm (also Luke 6:46-49).

We may compare these warnings to references to 'worthiness' in the matter of attaining to the resurrection or the age to come (Luke 20:35-36). Luke 20:35-36 speaks of godliness which is worthy of reward, and associates such reward with resurrection. Matthew 10:37-39 speaks of those who are not worthy and lose their lives. Luke 9:62 speaks of being unworthy of the kingdom. In Luke 12:35-

14. The disciples of the 'school of Shammai' especially used 'Gehinnom' of 'salvation through fire'; see J.Jeremias, *Theological Dictionary of the New Testament*, Eerdmans, 1964, Vol. 1, pp.657-658. I am not suggesting that this is the whole use of 'Gehenna'; Matthew 10:28; 23:15; 33; Luke 12:5 refer to something more serious. And of course there are places that speak of the eternal punishment of the lost without using the word 'Gehenna'. Paul does not use the word at all.

48, sayings concerning faithfulness include the parable of a servant who acts badly because he is not expecting his master's sudden return. When the master does return, the servant is put among the unfaithful and punished (Luke 12:46). There is variation in punishment according to knowledge of the master's will (Luke 12:47-48).

We are made to know, then, that we are dealing with a serious matter. Jesus refers to the right eye and the right hand. It is a way of speaking of something that is very precious to us and highly valued. What does a person value more than his hands and his eyes? The idea is that the Christian cuts out of his life something that is precious to him in order to protect his own purity.

These words are obviously not meant to be taken literally. Many of the phrases of the Sermon on the Mount are playful in their language. Nothing in the Sermon on the Mount uses the language of legislation. In the early church a theologian named Origen, when he was a young man, mutilated himself, thinking it necessary for his purity.[15] Later he realised his error and said that the Christian 'amputates the passions of the soul without touching the body'.[16]

Although these words are serious they are not to be made heavy or burdensome. Jesus' yoke is easy and his burden is light! The first aspect of 'cutting out the right eye' and 'cutting off the right hand' is to be rejoicing in God. Although it is a matter so serious that it will affect our reward in glory, yet actually obeying Jesus at this point

---

15. See Eusebius, *Ecclesiastical History* 6:8.
16. See his *Commentary on St. Matthew* (various editions), under Matthew 15:4.

involves our rejoicing in the Lord. One can do almost anything for God if one is rejoicing in the joy of knowing him.

We are to cut out of our lives those aspects which are specially tempting. It may be that a friendship has to fall aside. Certain types of books and newspapers will be rejected. We shall be choosy about what we allow our eyes to see. Sometimes it will be painful – like cutting out an eye or chopping off a hand. But we must do it. It is not that we withdraw from society. Luther had some good sense in commenting on these words.[17] 'Christ is not forbidding us to live together, to eat and drink, and even to laugh and have fun.' 'There are some people', says Luther, 'who have tightened it entirely too much and who want to be so holy that they forbid even a glance, and have taught that all companionship between men and women should be avoided'. He complains about those 'outstanding saints' who 'have run away from the world into the wilderness and into the monasteries'. There was nothing like that about Jesus. He had some surprising friends, men and women – and he was friendly to them even before they received his salvation!

Jesus is not referring to monasticism or isolationism. He expects us to be salt and light in the world. But no provision is to be made for the lusts of the flesh. What panders to the flesh and stimulates sin is to be ruthlessly cut out; the joy of the Lord will be our strength.

---

17. See M. Luther, *The Sermon on the Mount* (*Luther's Works*, vol. 21, Concordia, 1956), p.85.

12. Divorce
(Matthew 5:31-32)

Again, you have heard that it was said to the people of long ago, 'Whoever divorces his wife let him give her a certificate of divorce' (5:31), but I say to you that everyone who divorces his wife (except on the ground of unchastity) makes her commit adultery; and whoever marries a divorced woman commits adultery (5:32).

There must be three stages in our study of this crucial passage concerning divorce, if we are to be in any way practical in submitting to God's word.

(i) The first question is: what do these words mean (and what do the other passages which speak on the same subject mean – Matt. 19:3-12; Mark 10:2-12; Luke 16:18; 1 Cor. 7:10-16)? This is the *exegetical* stage.

(ii) There must be a second step. People who believe that the Bible presents a consistent, non-contradictory, teaching will want to press their researches forward until they discover the harmony of scripture. What must I believe? What is 'the bottom line', the teaching that I am to follow and teach. This is the *systematic-theological* stage.

(iii) There is a third stage. There must be *the pastoral consequences*. If one is a pastor, one cannot avoid the question: what then must I encourage (pray for, allow) among the people who seek my help? The 'shepherd' of God's people will be forced to ask himself *pastoral* questions.

1. *Consider the history of this matter*. Over the course of post-Reformation Protestant history most Bible-believing

Christians have been taught the 'Erasmian' view of marriage-and-divorce, first presented by Erasmus in 1519. This approach holds that immorality in one partner allows the other partner to divorce the guilty partner and entitles the 'innocent' partner to remarry. To this proviso a second was generally added. The 'Pauline privilege' of 1 Corinthians 7:15 says that when a Christian man or woman is deserted by his or her partner simply because the Christian is a Christian, the Christian is not obliged to hold on to the relationship but is 'not under bondage'. This too (it seems) allows remarriage.

A second approach is that of the early church which held the view that immorality in one partner or wilful desertion allows the other partner to divorce the guilty partner but does *not* justify remarriage. The earliest generations of Christians spoke Hellenistic Greek as their mother-tongue; so their interpretations of the Greek New Testament are always worthy of consideration. On the other hand, early Christian thinkers were much influenced by Platonism and this led them to be harshly negative in their views of marriage.

Thirdly, there are those who hold that the words 'except for immorality' give a reason why a marriage ought never to have occurred in the first place and 'divorce' is really only an annulment of something that never was legitimate. The New Jerusalem Bible translates Matthew 5:32 'except for the case of an illicit marriage'. The 'illicit marriage' entitling 'divorce' is viewed differently by different scholars and writers.[18]

---

18. (i) For some it is incestuous marriage (that is, the forbidden marriages within the relationships mentioned in Leviticus 18:6-18).

There are yet other approaches[19] but I must confine myself to supporting what I believe is right, and then hasten to the pastoral matters that are raised.

2. *Next, we must consider the teaching of the law.* The Mosaic law said: 'Whoever divorces his wife let him give her a certificate of divorce.' Deuteronomy 24:1-4 gave permission (not a command) for divorce on grounds of 'some indecency' and then it forbade her to return to her husband if she married another man after her divorce. It required a certificate of divorce to prove her entitlement to remarry. The second marriage was not adultery; it was not a breach of the seventh commandment. The law protected the *second* marriage in this case. 'Some indecency' seems to refer to behaviour of which society would disapprove.

(ii) For others it is marriage with non-Christians. (iii) Others think of immorality during the time of betrothal. (iv) Yet other interpreters think the 'immorality' consisted of Jewish-Gentile marriage forbidden by the Mosaic law.

19. There is (i) what has been called the 'preteritive' or 'no comment' view. This interprets the Greek phrase normally translated 'except on the grounds of unchastity' in an entirely different manner: 'leaving aside the matter of unchastity'. And there is (ii) the 'traditio-historical' approach which claims that the phrase 'except on the grounds of unchastity' was not originally found in Matthew's material but was added by Matthew himself to make life easier in the 'Matthean churches'. This view holds that Matthew's material is incoherent. (iii) Another approach, which originated with J.D.M. Derrett, believes that Matthew's point is that divorce followed by celibacy *must* take place after a wife has defiled herself by immorality. For the objections to these approaches, see W.A. Heth and G.J. Wenham, *Jesus and Divorce* (Paternoster) – an excellent study whether one agrees with it or not.

It did *not* specifically refer to adultery since in most cases that was punishable by death, not by divorce. Marriages with foreign women were forbidden altogether, and so divorce in such a situation was encouraged!

3. *Over against the law Jesus puts his teaching.* It is not legislation for magistrates. It deals with the heart and it deals with God's ideal. It is not an *impossible* ideal, but it is an *ideal* from which there might be lapses.

Jesus says: everyone who divorces his wife (except on the ground of unchastity) makes her commit adultery. The divorce *itself* creates adultery – whether she remarries or not – because it is a spiritual lapse from God's ideal. (One remembers how in the Old Testament serious sin is often called 'adultery'.[20]) It is 'adultery' in the sense of breaking one's commitments to God.

The words 'except on the ground of immorality' introduce an exception to the general forbidding of divorce. Where the other partner is guilty of such a serious destruction of the marriage, Jesus allows divorce without there being any shame or guilt. It is *not* a breach of one's commitment to God to 'divorce' in such circumstances.

It has been argued that the words 'except on the ground of immorality' in Matthew 19:9 do not belong to the words 'and marries another'. They *only* belong to the words 'whoever divorces his wife'. The sentence in Matthew 19:9 reads: *Whoever divorces his wife [except for immorality] and marries another* .... It does not read: *Whoever divorces his wife and marries another [except for immorality]*... This might give the impression that there is an exception

---

20. See Hosea 2:4; Jeremiah 5:7; Ezekiel 16:32, and elsewhere.

to the refusal of divorce but no exception to the refusal of remarriage. On this view divorce-and-remarriage is disallowed by Jesus, but in certain conditions separation is allowed.

However, Matthew 5:31-32 stands on its own *before* we read Matthew 19. At this point there is no question of an exceptive clause being placed *between* the mention of divorce and the mention of remarriage. Normally the word 'divorce' in itself implies remarriage. This would imply that there is an exception to Jesus' generally rejecting divorce and *also* an exception to his generally rejecting remarriage. Divorce *means* divorce-and-right-to-remarry. The idea of divorce-but-no-right-to-remarry is not the meaning of the word 'divorce'. On the early church view, Jesus would be re-defining the word 'divorce'. There is no independent evidence of this. It would make Jesus use the word 'divorce' in a way that is entirely unknown in the first century.

The point concerning the position of the exceptive clause in Matthew 19 is not as significant as might at first be thought. Matthew is a very Hebraistic Gospel and Hebraizing sentences tend to get the main points across speedily and then add further details. A notable example of such a Hebraistic style is Acts 16:31: 'Believe in the Lord Jesus Christ, and you will be saved – you and your household'. It is a Hebrew way of saying, 'If you and your household believe, you will all be saved'. But the Hebrew style gets the main point over speedily ('Believe in the Lord Jesus Christ, and you will be saved') and then adds the clarifying detail ('you and your household'). Something similar can be seen in Luke 19:44 (where 'and your children within you' is a delayed expression). Similarly Matthew 19:9 is in a hurry to put the exception ('Whoever divorces his wife – except for immorality...) and then gets on with the sentence. To think he is making a weighty point and redefining 'divorce' simply by the position of the clause is building too much on a linguistic detail. In Matthew 19:3 and 8 the word 'divorce' has already been used in the traditional way; there is no hint of a changed meaning in 19:9.

Jesus' main point is not to approve of divorce but to make the point that in at least one situation divorce is not to be regarded as unfaithfulness to God. In a situation of sexual disloyalty divorce is not disapproved of by Jesus.

Jesus continues: '...and whoever marries a divorced woman commits adultery'. Jesus is not redefining the word 'divorce' but he is redefining the word 'adultery'! 'Adultery' for Jesus means any form of sexual disloyalty, which is at one and the same time disloyalty to God.

4. We must now come – if our study is to be applied and obeyed – to what I have called above stages two and three: the difficult question of the harmony of biblical teaching and how it should be applied in pastoral practice. The two matters affect each other; I comment on them together.

A lot depends on whether Jesus' teaching here is taken as 'law' comparable to the law of Moses. If it is some kind of legislation, there is difficulty in harmonizing Jesus' words here (which mention divorce on one ground only) with the teaching of Mark 10:2-12 and Luke 16:18 (which discourage divorce altogether and mention no exceptions) and with 1 Corinthians 7:10-16 (which mentions another ground for divorce not mentioned in the Gospels). How does one find agreement or harmony in all of this?

My own view is that the Sermon on the Mount is not legislation at all. Its prescriptions cannot be turned into laws. How could one make a 'law' about the beatitudes? Or about 'turning the other cheek'? Does one *really* give one's coat to anyone who asks. (I have been asked for items of my clothing often on the East African coast where 'beach-boys' like to be paid for their sea-shells in clothing which they then sell. But I have never yet given much to those who have wanted my shirt!) Jesus' teaching is surely about attitudes and what Paul would later call 'living in the Spirit'. The impulse of the Spirit and the appeal of Jesus is: we should hate divorce. But the very disagreements in the 'divorce texts' show that Jesus is generalizing. Jesus was *generalizing* when he said, 'Make no oath at all' for he himself was willing to take an oath (see 26:63-64 – in this same Gospel). Mark 10:2-12 and Luke 16:18 refer to similar *generalizing*. When one is *generalizing* exact agreement is not needed. It is clear that Jesus leads us *away* from divorce. Mark and Luke mention no exceptions. There may indeed be exceptions but Mark and Luke are *generalizing*. Matthew tells of how Jesus himself mentioned an obvious exception. Paul mentioned another situation where there is obviously an exception.

So now there is an obvious question: might there be *further* exceptions? There are two matters here: (i) what are God's ideals for marriage and divorce? And (ii) how does one cope when God's ideals are broken?

God's ideal plan is certainly that marriage be lifelong and that neither separation nor divorce take place (Mark

10:2-9; Matt. 19:3-8). Divorce is never an ideal, always a second best. Divorce followed by remarriage is failure comparable (though not exactly identical) to the breaking of the seventh commandment. It is 'adultery' newly defined by Jesus (Matt. 5:32b; Mark 10:11-12; Luke 16:18). Married couples should ideally not separate or divorce – ever (1 Cor. 7:10). In cases of separation or divorce the people concerned must remain single or be reconciled (1 Cor. 7:11).

But the question is, might there be additional 'exceptions' where divorce followed by remarriage is permissible? My answer to this is: yes! Jesus mentioned one. Paul mentions another. Could there be other 'exceptions' to the Sermon on the Mount, just as there are to the rulings about oaths and the giving of the coat? These refer more to the heart than to legislation. Consider this situation. There are two unsaved couples, Mr. and Mrs A; and Mr. and Mrs B. Both marriages break up. There is multiple immorality by all the partners after both of their marriages have broken up. Both marriages end in divorce. All partners are sexually 'guilty parties'. Then Mr. A meets Mrs B. They 'fall in love'. They get married and become Mr. and Mrs C. They have three children and are reasonably happy. Then one day they are invited to a Christian meeting. Mr. and Mrs C (who once were Mr. A and Mrs B) come to experience salvation in Christ. Soon they are asking questions about the validity of their marriage. They were both divorced. Now that they have discovered that their original divorces were sinful and that their marriage as Mr. and Mrs C was adulterous. 'Whoever marries a divorced woman commits adultery'. Are Mr.

and Mrs C now living in life-long adultery? Must they find their original partners and send their children to different homes? Of course not! The Sermon on the Mount was not intended as legislation to be ridiculously applied. One does not ridiculously 'turn the other cheek' and one cannot always literally apply Jesus' words about divorce as if they were 'legislation'. What should Mr. and Mrs C do about their marriage with such dubious origins? I answer: nothing! There is surely no need to break up what is now a long-standing marriage. What would happen to the children of Mr. and Mrs C if Mr. C tried to find his previous partner, Mrs A? Is Mrs C to try to reconnect with her partner (Mr. B) of many years ago? Of course not!

Sometimes I am asked, Pastor, what do you think of divorce? I answer: It is like the question, what do you think of murder? I am against it! But if I am asked the question, 'Can a murderer be forgiven and start life again?' I answer: Yes! And if I am asked, 'Is there ever a time when it might be necessary to take someone's life?', I answer, 'I can imagine some situations where it might be right' (capital punishment? a war involving national self-defence? a situation where either mother or child is certain to lose a life but one life can be saved? the loss of one life for the saving of many lives?). It could be the lesser of two evils.

And if I am asked: 'Is there ever a time when it might be best to divorce?', I answer 'Well, the biblical ideal is against it, but I can imagine situations where it would be the lesser of two evils.' A person 'walking in the Spirit' will be willing in principle to be smitten again and again – but will not regard Matthew 5:39 as legislation. Similarly a person 'walking in the Spirit' will know how much Jesus hates divorce. But as Jesus, and Paul, said, there will be exceptions. There will be times when a marriage was dead and buried years ago, but now the person concerned wants to start a Christian marriage. Do I approve of divorce? Well, do I approve of murder? No – to both questions! Can a murderer be forgiven? Can a divorcee start again? Yes – to both questions! Is it ever right to take a life? I can imagine situations where it would be the lesser of two evils. Would it ever be right to allow a divorcee to remarry? Yes – just as a forgiven murderer may start life again in Jesus.

The principle is: Jesus' standards are high! But the power of God's grace is high also! Jesus will not lower the standards of his will. But his grace is truly amazing, and all sorts of sinners have been given a fresh start – including divorcees.

13. Simple Talk
(Matthew 5:33-37)

Jesus now moves on to our speech. There was not much legislation in the law about our talk. Jesus could perhaps have quoted the ninth commandment, but he now goes outside the Ten Commandments and chooses to comment on the legislation concerning oath-taking.

Often in modern English, 'to swear' means to use curses or filthy language, but the word here means insisting that what one is saying is true and at the same time inviting God to bring judgment if what one says is not true. It is when a person says something like, 'I swear by God that what I am saying is true.'

1. First, let us consider the law. The law encouraged oath-taking. Deuteronomy 6:13 said, 'You shall fear Yahweh your God, and serve him, and swear by his name.' At certain times oaths were required (see Exod. 22:11; Num. 5:19, 21). All covenant-making had oath-taking at its heart. 'Take an oath' and 'make a covenant' are identical ideas. There could be no covenant without oath.

Jesus says, *Again, you have heard that it was said to the people of long ago, 'You shall not swear falsely, but you shall perform to the Lord what you have sworn'* (5:33). The 'quotation' is not a precise quotation but a summary of the kind of instruction we have in Leviticus 19:12 ('Do not swear falsely by my name...'), Numbers 30:2 ('When a man makes a vow to Yahweh or takes an oath ... he must not break his word...'), Deuteronomy 23:21-23 ('If you make a vow ... do not be slow to pay it...'). Change of mind after an oath was regarded as serious sin (see Ps. 15:1, 4). 'Swear falsely' means 'break an oath' or 'be guilty of falsehood by not keeping an oath'.

2. Next, consider Jesus' scorn of the oath-taking habits of his own day. It seems that oath-taking had become a disgrace in Jesus' time. Jewish people in the first century often took oaths but instead of saying, 'I swear by God', they would say, 'I swear by heaven' or 'I swear by the earth' or 'by Jerusalem' or 'by my head'. This was thought to be not 'really' swearing. It was (so they thought) a kind of lesser oath-taking and did not require such care as swearing by God! But Jesus condemns the entire business of greater and lesser 'oath-taking'. *But I say to you, 'Do not swear at all, either by heaven, for it is the throne of*

God (5:34), *or by earth, for it is his footstool, or by Jerusalem, for it is the city of the great King* (5:35). *And do not swear by your head, for you cannot make one hair white or black'* (5:36). Jesus scorns the idea that one can make oaths that are unimportant because they do not use the word 'God' (see Matt. 23:16-22 for some similar words).

As always in the Sermon on the Mount Jesus is generalizing. His words are not absolute law. On rare occasions oath-taking might be a good idea. The other person needs it, perhaps. Jesus himself took an oath in a law-court (Matt. 26:63). Oaths are found in the New Testament (Rom. 1:9; 2 Cor. 1:18, 23; 1 Thess. 2:5, 10; Gal. 1:20). The greatest oath-taker in the Bible is God himself. He often 'swears by his holiness'.

But generally, oath-taking and other comparable extremes of self-centred declamations of one's own truthfulness are to be avoided.

Oath-taking 'protests too much'. It is implicitly claiming a high level of sincerity and integrity – as if one never was guilty of exaggeration or could not conceivably say anything misleading or hypocritical. It is claiming a kind of super-spiritual truthfulness that few of us actually have. If we are as truthful as that, we do not have to emphasize the point!

Oath-taking implies a double standard of truth. It is in effect saying, 'I am not always bothered about telling the truth but at this point I really am!' But if we have to insist that we are telling the truth *now*, then what is happening at other times? Jesus wants us to adopt a standard of truth-telling which is our style of talk all the time. We need to

91

defend ourselves less and let God bring the truth out in his own time and manner.

3. Next, consider what Jesus requires of his disciples. He demands utterly simple and straightforward ways of talking. *Let what you say be simply 'Yes' or 'No'; everything more than this comes from the evil one* (5:37). Christian talk should be straightforward. We should generally be able to give straight answers to a yes/no question. Christian talk should be simple, undefensive.

Often it means that we have to be willing to take accusation and slander and to receive unjust blame. Careless talk generally arises in situations where we feel we are being unjustly treated. Then we lash out in something that comes close to oath-taking. Some might even say, 'I swear to God I did not do this or that...' It is the accusation or slander that tempts us to over-statement or even to use God's name in our quarrels. But we must remember Jesus. Was he not the greatest example of someone being blamed for something he had not done? He was 'blamed' by God the Father for the sins of the whole world. He was treated by God and by men as if he had sinned. If we really are to be like Jesus, we must be willing to take false blame without reacting in an oath-taking manner. Jesus stayed cool despite sarcasm. '*We were not born of fornication,*' they said to him – hinting sarcastically that he was! Obviously, rumours of the virgin conception of Jesus had got to them. I think I might have said, 'Nor was I' and rushed to defend myself! Jesus did not react in that way. He avoided oath-taking or defensive protestations of his own righteousness.

'The power of life and death are in the tongue' (Prov. 18:21). Jesus says: Let what you say be simply 'Yes' or 'No'. Simple statements, simple denials, simple straight-forward explanations. 'Those who guard their lips guard their lives' (Prov. 13:3). Personally I have started to pray every day, 'Set a guard over my mouth, O LORD; keep watch over the door of my lips' (Ps. 141:3). Actually there are many promises that God will help us in this. 'I will be with your mouth and teach you what to say', said God to Moses (Exod. 4:12). He was referring to Moses' prophetic gift as leader of Israel, but if God can put the right words into the lips of the prophets, surely he can do something similar for each of his disciples. 'The Holy Spirit will teach you what to say,' promised Jesus to his disciples when they were to be brought before persecuting authorities (Luke 12:12). Surely he can do the same before a persecuting wife, a persecuting husband, a persecuting employer or a slanderous enemy.

Everything more than this comes from the evil one. The devil is at work in all careless talk. It is an area of life where he loves to be diligent! The tongue is a fire), a wild animal, a deadly poison (Jam. 3:6-8), and often the devil lies behind our attempts to achieve our own ends by our talk.

But silence is not always the answer! Jesus said, *Let what you say be simply 'Yes' or 'No'.* He did not say we should say nothing! Actually silence is sometimes the mark of the wicked. 'The wicked are silenced in darkness' (1 Sam. 2:9). Jesus told the unclean spirit to be silent (see Mark 1:25). Silence can be from the devil as well as too much talk! The Christian is not simply a person who says

93

nothing. There is no great wisdom in never saying anything. Jesus was silent under accusation, but he had plenty to say at other times. Christian control of the tongue is not simply keeping silent – although that is often needed under provocation. It is not silence but 'a word fitly spoken' that is 'like apples of gold' (Prov. 25:11).

How do we get to be like this? A lot depends on whether we really believe in the sovereignty of God. Oftentimes we talk too rashly because we do not really believe God is in control. We are trying to *achieve* something by our wild talk that is best left to God. If we believe in prayer more, in the sovereignty of God more, our 'Yes' would more often be 'Yes'. Our 'No' would more often be 'No'.

14. Turning the Other Cheek
(Matthew 5:38-42)

Six times in Matthew 5:21-48, Jesus says 'You have heard that it was said ... But I say to you'. The fifth occasion, found in Matthew 5:38-42, is the most difficult to take literally. *You have heard that it was said, 'An eye for an eye and a tooth for a tooth* (5:38)...

We have seen that certain principles become obvious as these contrasts with the Mosaic law are considered.

(i) None of Jesus' recommendations is to be precisely found in the Mosaic law. They all go far beyond the law or even change the Mosaic law quite sharply.

(ii) None of them is 'legislation'. Jesus himself did not refrain from taking oaths.

(iii) Jesus is dealing with personal attitudes more than making hard-and-fast rules.

94

(iv) They are not to be taken with total literalness. Origen, who mutilated himself, might be thought to be obeying Matthew 5:29, but he made a mistake.

In this section another obvious principle stands out: (v) Jesus is dealing more with the individual than with law for society. One notices how the plural 'you' in verse 38 becomes a singular 'you' in verses 39-42. Jesus deals here with personal relationships and attitudes.

The Russian nobleman, social reformer and novelist, Count Leo Nikolaevitch Tolstoy, became famous for his taking these words of Jesus in (as he thought) 'the exact sense in which he uses them'.[21] He was horrified to find religious people who seemed not to be bothered about mass murder in war. He questioned scientists and priests looking for an answer to life's enigmas. He studied Chinese, Buddhist and Moslem scriptures but came to believe that the Sermon on the Mount should be applied to every aspect of life with the strictest literal interpretation. 'Christ meant exactly what he said,' thought Tolstoy, and Matthew 5:39 is (he argued) the key to the Sermon on the Mount and the key to life itself.

We must admire Tolstoy's sincerity, and pity him in his painful quest for meaning in life – a quest which, for him, was never satisfied. But his ultra-literal interpretation was always impractical, even for himself. At one stage he temporarily abandoned attempts to interpret Jesus' teaching because of the difficulties it was leading him into.

---

21. I lean here on the 26-page survey of Tolstoy's teaching, in C.Bauman, *The Sermon on the Mount: The Modern Quest for Its Meaning* (Mercer University Press, 1985). Full references to Tolstoy's writings are given there.

He made at least the following mistakes:

(i) he thought he admired Jesus' teaching but he never took seriously the way Jesus draws attention to himself in the Sermon on the Mount.

(ii) The Sermon on the Mount is not a book of 'commandments'.

(iii) Tolstoy had to struggle with the fact that a totally literal interpretation of Matthew 5:39 destroys any kind of order in society, especially if it is used in civic legislation!

(iv) Tolstoy's 'religion' was totally confined to 'morality', and morality alone brings salvation neither to the individual nor to society. His approach (and with it that of his admirers like the Indian lawyer, Ghandi, and books like Charles Sheldon's Pelagian[22] novel, *In His Steps*) has to be entirely left aside.

1. Again Jesus begins by recalling the Mosaic legislation. He quotes the words of Exodus 21:24, Leviticus 24:20 and Deuteronomy 19:21. *You have heard that it was said, 'An eye for an eye and a tooth for a tooth...'* The famous ruling of Exodus 21:24 was a piece of law dealing with accidental injury and what compensation should be paid when one person injured another. The ruling was intended to control and limit revenge. The point of it was that no *more* than the value of an eye should be taken for an injury to the eye, and so on. The offending party should not be killed in revenge, but only the true value of the

---

22. Pelagianism was the fifth century heresy which taught that people could reach high levels of godliness with minimal experience of God's grace.

injury could be received in compensation. Exodus 21:30 suggests that such a penalty could be turned into a financial payment, when the injured person agreed. There is evidence that such transfers of value were permitted (compare Exodus 21:26; 36:6 where such transfers are made). There is no evidence that literal mutilation was an acceptable punishment in Old Testament times in Israel. Only in the case of wilful murder was it impossible to transfer a penalty like this into its cash equivalent (see Num. 35:31).

This interpretation of the law is put beyond doubt when it is seen that 'life for life' cannot mean that the life was literally taken, because the law did not demand the death penalty in the case of accidental killing.

So the law allowed a kind of legal revenge – the payment of a fine – but made sure it was not excessive.

2. Next, Jesus again puts his own demand. There is no reason to think (contrary to some expositions) that Jesus is referring to a *misuse* of the Mosaic law. Perhaps people in the first century did misuse this ruling of the law and used it to justify vindictive attitudes. It is quite likely. But there is actually no statement in the text to this effect and Jesus' words, 'An eye for an eye and a tooth for a tooth' are a quite adequate summary of the law itself. Jesus did not exactly speak against the law. It still is a good legal principle; legal retribution must not be excessive. Jesus simply put his own demand in contrast to the legal principle of the Mosaic law. In personal relationships Jesus' disciples are invited to outstrip the law. The law was adequate as a statement of a principle of justice for the

days of Moses, but the disciples must get far beyond mere 'principles of justice'. They must be able to control their attitudes. Jesus requires total freedom from a vindictive spirit: *but I say to you: do not resist[23] the evil person.* We recognize that the person showing hatred is an 'evil person' in what he or she does, but we refuse any kind of spirit of vengeance.

Jesus refers to four areas of life where we tend to become exceedingly bitter about ill-treatment.

(i) Violent insult. *On the contrary, if anyone strikes you on the right cheek, turn to him the other cheek also* (5:39). The 'right cheek' suggests that what is in mind is the back-handed slap on the cheek given as a deliberate insult.

(ii) False accusation in court. *And if someone wishes to take you to court to get your tunic, allow him also to have the outer garment* (5:40). The law allowed the inner garment to be confiscated in certain situations but never the outer garment (Exod. 22:26-27).

(iii) Oppression by colonial military authorities. *And if anyone legally demand that you go with him one mile, go with him two miles!* (5:41). Roman soldiers, a foreign occupying power, were allowed to demand that people they met on the road carry their military equipment. Jesus' teaching clearly refers to one-to-one relationships, yet verse 41 also lets us know that Jesus was not a revolutionary.

(iv) Unfair demands. *Give to the person demanding*

---

23. It is sometimes thought that *antistenai* refers to taking fellow believers to court. I once took it this way myself but now see that the four examples given demand a wider meaning.

something from you, and do not turn away from the one
wishing to borrow something from you (5:42).

In all four areas of life Jesus requires that in our personal
relationships we shun any spirit of retaliation. None of
them should be turned into legislation. We need not give
money to drunkards or to the many 'street boys' of the
world's cities. Protest against aggression is not forbidden
(see John 18:22-23).

But when one has said what it does *not* mean, Matthew
5:38-42 remains one of the highest challenges of Scripture.
We think of occasions when people insult us, when we
face false accusation, when someone does his best to get
us into trouble, when enemies want to squeeze the last
drop of our finances from us, when former business
associates take us to court and tell the most outrageous
lies, when government officials are infuriating and unfair
in their demands, when relatives pressurize us for money
beyond our ability to cope, when someone deliberately
sets themselves up in rivalry to what we are wanting to
do. One thinks of the unfair situations found in Scripture.
'I have done nothing to justify my being put in this prison,'
– said Joseph (Gen. 40:15). Jonathan asked his father King
Saul, 'Why will you put David to death without a cause?'
(1 Sam. 19:5). 'They hated me without a cause,' said Jesus,
taking Psalm 35:19 and applying David's words to himself
(John 15:25).

The saints of God suffer in situations that tempt them
to the deepest imaginable bitterness – but then Jesus says
to such, 'Do nothing about it. Leave it to me. Don't take
vengeance. Leave your case and your cause in my hands.'
It is not a strict law. Sometimes we must take necessary

99

and reasonable steps to handle injustice, sometimes for the sake of others, sometimes even for the sake of our enemy. Jesus addresses the heart more than he makes a law. In our hearts we have to be willing to leave our case and our cause entirely with God. We do what is the best thing to be done, led by his Holy Spirit. It may be some kind of confrontation will be necessary. Matthew 5:39 is not a law written on tablets on stone. But what is to be written on our hearts is an entire willingness to leave vengeance with God. Matthew 5:39 deals with the spirit. Often it will not be taken with total literalness. But then sometimes God's Holy Spirit will require exactly that: that we do nothing and leave justice and vindication entirely and exclusively to God. It might be agonizingly painful. We may have to get down on our knees and plead for God's grace.

This is not the way to run an army or a police force or even a business – but it is the way to find the approval of God. And when we do nothing in self-defence, we may find that God does everything. Joseph became second only to Pharaoh. David became king in place of Saul. And Jesus, who did not resist Judas, and who was struck on the cheek, and who endured false charges in court and emptied himself of his very life – has been exalted as King of the universe.

15. Hatred and Love
(Matthew 5:43-48)

It is not surprising that the last of the six contrasts in Matthew 5:21-48 deals with love. When the Pharisees were

100

free to say whatever they liked they would often ask questions about law (see Matt. 22:34-40). When Jesus felt free to say whatever he liked he would talk about himself (see Matt. 22:41-45) or he would present the need of love. The six contrasts of 5:21-48 end with love, and so does the Sermon on the Mount as a whole, as we shall see (in Matt. 7:12).

1. Again Jesus begins with the Old Testament legislation. *You have heard that it was said 'You shall love your neighbour and hate your enemy'* (5:43). The first words, 'You shall love your neighbour', echo Leviticus 19:18. The words, 'and hate your enemy', are not precisely to be found in the Old Testament. Here is the best case – it might be thought – for thinking Jesus is only correcting first century perversions of the law and not the law itself. But even here the case is weak! Jesus' positive instructions have in fact departed from the law *itself,* not just from perversions of it. Hard evidence that first century Jews *taught* the hatred of enemies is difficult to find – although their hatred of foreigners was real enough. It is an unproven assumption that they *taught* hatred. The words of Matthew 5:43 are probably still simply summarising the Mosaic law. Deuteronomy gave instructions that demanded what could (in comparison to love required towards a neighbour) be called 'hatred' of Israel's Canaanite enemies. When David said, 'I hate them with perfect hatred' (Ps. 139:22), he was being loyal to the legislation concerning Israel's enemies. Pagan nations were to be exterminated (Deut. 7:1). They were to be 'destroyed' – wiped out of existence, exterminated (7:2). Marriage with them was forbidden

(7:3). The implements of their religion were to be smashed or destroyed by fire (7:5). The Mosaic law certainly demanded that Canaanites be treated with utmost severity. 'Hate your enemy' is a fair summary of what should be Israel's attitude to the Canaanites, as required by the Mosaic law. First century Jewish teaching no doubt exploited this strand of the law (one thinks of the way the Samaritans were hated), but the law itself encouraged it in some ways. Those who think 'Hate your enemies' is a blatant perversion of the law have not paid sufficient attention to details of what the law says! And they are ironing out the differences between Exodus–Deuteronomy and the Sermon on the Mount. Jesus 'fulfils' the law, but does so by presenting demands that are at times quite different from the law.

2. Jesus' requirement for his disciples 'fulfils the law' but is different in detail. He presents a sharp contrast to this particular detail of the law: *but I say to you: love your enemies, and pray for those who persecute you* (5:44).

The highest achievement of the Christian is to love his or her enemies: those who cause us suffering, those who oppose us, those who block our way to achievement or fulfilment, those who slander or criticize, those who want to get us into trouble, the discourteous, the vindictive, the man or woman who is sarcastic or brutal or malicious, or who in rivalry wants to take to themselves something that has been ours.

We are asked to love them. It will involve 'laying down our lives', sacrificing time and energy for others. It will involve compassion, relating to people in the way Jesus

related to his contemporaries (who were not always smooth
and polite!). It will involve kindness, patience, graciousness, endurance, humility. It will be freedom from jealousy,
envy, roughness, criticism. It will be persistence in
goodwill. Yet at the same time this 'love' of Jesus will
not be sentimental, sloppy, feigned, artificial, patronizing.
Many think they are showing love when in fact they are
being patronizing. Love does not want the other person to
feel patronized – a special difficulty in areas of social or
economic inequality.

A special test of whether we love our enemies is whether
we pray for them. It is easy to put on a display of showing
love to enemies, when secretly we sometimes feel quite
different. The test is secret intercession. What we pray for
reveals how we truly feel about others. Jesus asks us to
pray for our worst enemies as if they were our best friends.
He wants us to take upon our shoulders the needs and
difficulties and problems of our worst critics, our cruelest
tormentors – and pray for them as we would our greatest
friends.

3. Jesus puts likeness to God as a spiritual goal. It is this
kind of prayerfulness towards our enemies that brings us
to be close to God in character. Pray, Jesus says, for those
who persecute you, *so that you may be children of your
Father who is in heaven. For he causes the sun to rise on
the righteous and the unrighteous* (5:45). God himself is
incredible in his love towards enemies. There are those
who oppose God, who resist his attempts to bring salvation
to the world. There are those who slander and criticize
him! They are discourteous to him, sarcastic about him.

103

They do not give thanks to him or glorify him as God. But God loves his enemies! We are being truly 'godly' – God-like – when we 'so love the world' as God did.

Children represent their father. One of the main functions of a son is representation. A father (in the ancient world, and today in rural undeveloped areas of the world) will send his son on a mission to represent him. Jesus was the 'Son' of God in the greatest sense imaginable. 'He who has seen me has seen the Father,' Jesus said. In a lesser sense (much lesser!) the Christian should be able to say, 'He who has seen me, has seen the Father.' It is an awe-inspiring thought. We are to be 'children' of God, representing God our heavenly Father.

Of course, in some ways we are not to be like God at all. We do not portray the wrath of God, or the omniscience of God. Unlike our Father, we do not fill all space. We are not from everlasting to everlasting. We are not God-like in these matters. Jesus has already told us (in Matt. 5:38-42) to leave these aspects of God's character to him! Vengeance is his; we do not have to represent him in his vengeance (unless we are civic officials – Rom. 13:4). But we represent him in his love towards his enemies. God treats his enemies and his friends alike: *He causes the sun to rise on the righteous and the unrighteous*. Imagine a world where the sun shone only on the righteous and clouds hung over the heads of the unrighteous. Imagine a world where righteous farmers got rain from heaven but unrighteous farmers got no rain for their crops! But God is not like that; he is amazing in his love towards enemies.

He is that way in salvation too! He sent Jesus for 'whoever' would believe in him. He sent Jesus to the cross to taste death for every person. If God is like that, we are asked to be the same, so as to represent God in this world.

4. Jesus gives the arguments for what he says. Jesus is not anti-intellectual. He often appeals to our minds and gives us reasoned arguments for what he presses upon us. He does not resemble a philosopher in *trusting* the mind overmuch, but he still asks people to think! *For if you love those who love you, what reward do you have? Do not even the tax collectors do the same? (5:46) And if you greet your brothers only, what do you do more than other people? Do not even the Gentiles do the same? (5:47).*

The Christian is meant to be different. We can all love our friends! Only the grace of God enables us truly to treat our worst enemies and our best friends alike – in our prayers and intercessions.

5. Jesus comes to a conclusion. *Therefore you are to be perfect, as your heavenly Father is perfect (5:48).* Does Jesus really mean this? Can we really be 'perfect'? Is it just a distant far-off goal? What does he mean? He cannot mean 'sinlessly' perfect. We shall never reach the point in this world where we do not need to pray daily, 'Forgive us our trespasses.' We shall never get to the point where we can say to God, 'I do not need the blood of Jesus today because I did not sin!' We shall always need the blood of Jesus Christ, and Jesus himself to be our 'Advocate with the Father'.

'Perfection' is all-round maturity – and we are not getting anywhere near it until we love our enemies. We are to be 'perfect' – having every area of our life pleasing to God. Does anyone ever reach it in this life? No and yes – in that order! No! If anyone thinks he is without sin, he deceives himself. But yes! When we are able to hear his voice and be taught by him (see 1 Cor. 2:6; 14:20; Phil. 3:15), we have reached a level of spirituality which is 'complete'; it has every area of life pleasing to God. God can still see faults in us but he is pleased with every department of our lives. When we are able to distinguish God's will for our lives (Heb. 5:14), able to endure in trial (Jas. 1:12), able to control our tongue (Jas. 3:2), able to cast out fear (1 John 4;18), able to let God be totally in charge of our level of wealth (see Matt. 19:21), and able to love our enemies[24] – then we have not reached total sinlessness, we are not angels in disguise, but we are – even in this life – pleasing to God. I do not think anyone would be wise to claim to have reached it, but the command still stands: *you are to be perfect, as your heavenly Father is perfect.* Thank God that the blood of Christ is there for our pardon as well. What would we do without it? Fortunately for us, his perfect love casts out our fear – otherwise we would live in terror of not being perfect. Be perfect! But start by having faith in the perfect faithfulness of Jesus. The first thing God wants from us in our quest for 'perfection' is faith in the cleansing blood of his Son.

---

24. The Greek word *teleios* is used in these references. It is used also in Eph. 4:13. This kind of 'perfection' was the aim of Paul's ministry (Col. 1:28; 4:12).

16. Keeping Our Eyes on God
(Matthew 6:1-4)

The Sermon on the Mount takes a new direction in Matthew 6:1. Jesus began by describing the disciples (5:3-16). Then he explained that he fulfils the law of God; and went on to say what this would mean for the disciples' relationship to the Mosaic covenant (5:17-48). They do not directly relate to it at all! By the time we have reached Matthew 5:48 we see that what Jesus is doing is redirecting our obedience exclusively towards himself. Under the covenant with Moses, the believer related to God via Moses and the blood of the passover lamb. 'This book of the law shall not depart out of your mouth ...' was the great commission of the Mosaic epoch (Josh. 1:8). 'Teaching them to observe everything I – I myself – have commanded you...' is the great demand of the New Covenant relationship to Jesus, inaugurated by Jesus' own blood. Jesus 'fulfils' the law, and then redirects his disciples attention to himself for ever after. They will also fulfil the law, but they will do it by attending to his commands.

Now Jesus goes a stage further. Old Covenant believers related to God; Moses-and-the-law was a kind of mediator between them and God. Now Jesus alone is the mediator. He brings his disciples to God through himself. So this means that the disciples are to go through life with their eye on God. Jesus died, the just for the unjust, 'to bring us to God' (1 Pet. 3:18).

The rest of the Sermon on the Mount is developing this thought. Matthew 6:1-18 could be entitled: Living in the

Sight of God. Matthew 6:19-33 could be entitled: Living on the Provision of God. Matthew 7:1-27 could be entitled: Living under the Judgment of God.

Matthew 6:1-18 looks at our spiritual life (giving to the needy, prayer, fasting), focusing upon the way we relate to others (giving, 6:2-4), the way we relate to God (prayer, 6:5-15) and the way we relate to ourselves (the self-discipline of fasting, 6:16-18) .

Then the thought moves to God as our provider, looking at two possible attitudes towards possessions and wealth, greed (6:19-24) or anxiety (6:25-34). Greed and anxiety are both symptoms of a failure to keep one's eye on God.

Then – as we shall see – the thought moves to the future, and to what it means to live in the expectation of the judgment of God.

1. First, we have a general principle: his disciples are to reject a wrong kind of motivation. Jesus says, *Take care not to perform your righteousness in front of men and women, in order to be seen by them; otherwise you will have no reward from your Father who is in heaven* (6:1). Part of the crookedness that is to be found in human nature is our desire for honour and glory. Man was created in the image of God but then sinned and today 'lacks the glory of God' (Rom. 3:23). Yet it seems that we can hardly bear to live without glory. We all want people to admire us and appreciate us. Those who are starved of appreciation have personality problems. Some are obvious in their egotistical self-centredness. Others are equally full of self-pleasing hunger for appreciation, but they are rather more subtle about it – and all the more likely to deceive themselves

into thinking that others are self-centred but they are not!

A great spiritual challenge comes to us when we consider how we are to recover our lost glory. Jesus' teaching is that we are not to get our lost glory from each other but we are to get it from God. We are not to perform our righteousness in front of others so as to get them to admire us. I suppose we all like receiving praise. It is encouraging when someone expresses their appreciation of us or of something we have done. But we had best keep ourselves from getting addicted to praise because if we love it too much it damages us. If we actually begin to do good deeds with the intention of getting a reputation for ourselves, then we get no reward for whatever we did, none whatsoever. Such 'good deeds' are totally discounted by God as worthless.

We must balance this verse with Matthew 5:16. There Jesus says we are to let our light shine before others so that they may see our good works and give glory to our Father who is in heaven. A city situated on the top of a hill cannot be hidden. God has not given us a spirit of timidity! People see that Christian people are different and they start taking notice.

There is a balance here. Everything hinges on motivation and intention. What is needed is boldness in doing God's will – but boldness with total self-forgetfulness and dedication to God. God wants us to care very little of what others think of us – or even of what we think of ourselves!

2. Next, Jesus gives three examples, beginning with financial help for the needy. Jesus expects us to help needy people. *'For example,'* he says: *'When you give financial*

109

help for the needy, do not sound a trumpet before you as
the hypocrites do in the synagogues and in the streets, so
that they may be admired by other people. Truly I say to
you, they have their reward (6:2). But when you give
financial help for the needy do not let your right hand
know what your left hand is doing (6:3), so that your giving
to the needy may be in secret, and then your Father who
sees in secret will reward you' (6:4).

Jesus will bring us into contact with people who need
our help. We need to be careful. There are people around
who are very clever at getting money out of sweet but
gullible Christians. Before we give help to people in this
way there needs to be detailed knowledge of the other
person's need. Unthinking benevolence does more harm
than good. People that like playing at being benefactors,
without wisdom or skill, often are a nuisance and bring all
sorts of crooks to the doors of the church! But still –
simpletons and crooks aside – Jesus expects us to help
needy people, sensibly, wisely, knowledgeably,
beneficially, constructively, generously.

3. Jesus tells us how not to do it. It must be totally without
seeking attention for oneself: do not sound a trumpet before
you. There are some people – and perhaps we have been
among them – who before they do anything generous like
to sound a blast on a trumpet to announce what they are
doing. The words are only· imagery and picture language.
There is no evidence that any literal trumpet-blowing was
done. Reference to the 'synagogue' and 'streets' refers to
actual practices in Jesus' day. Obviously, generous people
were publicly recognized in the synagogues. Or the person

known to be generous would be greeted on the streets. But Jesus says giving of this kind must be secret.

What a lot of God's blessing gets lost by self-advertizement. Christian donors to needy causes lose much by telling the news to the world! Sometimes announcements are given telling how much has been given to the church by this person or that person. Sometimes the news will appear on television: 'Mr. So-And-So went to a function and he gave this amount to a worthy cause.' The whole world is told!

4. Christian mercy of this kind must be without advertizement or self-consciousness, says Jesus. Not only do you not tell others what you are doing, you don't even tell yourself! 'Do not let your right hand know what your left hand is doing.' This is Jesus' playful and humorous way of speaking of our deliberately not focusing overmuch on what we are doing. We do it as unto God – and then we forget about it.

5. The Christian looks to the right kind of reward at the right time from the right person. The theme of reward runs through these verses: '... otherwise you will have no reward from your Father ... they have their reward ... then your Father who sees in secret will reward you'. What is the reward? It seems that it is largely honour. What we want from men and women is honour and glory. We are not to seek for it that way, but we shall get it from God! There is no reward from God if we are determined to get praise from men and women.

Reward is an obvious theme of the Bible, although we

tend to be fearful that the idea of salvation by grace alone contradicts the idea of reward. But there is no difficulty so long as we insist that the reward is not salvation. This would be a serious misunderstanding: salvation does *not* come to us as a reward. Reward is something over-and-above our salvation. It is given to us in God's mercy as an encouragement for us to live for him. In the New Testament the theme explicitly begins here, in the Sermon on the Mount. A particular kind of life brings blessedness (Matt. 5:3-12). Reward comes as we live for God alone, inwardly living for the 'Well done' of God. Generosity to the needy is rewarded (6:3-4). Secret prayerfulness is rewarded (6:5-15). Fasting is rewarded, when it is done in God's will and as a means to serving him (6:16-18). It can never be wrong to live for *God's* reward.

(i) The reward has a lot to do with Jesus expressing his pleasure in us. It can never be wrong to seek honour from Jesus.

(ii) The reward is a spiritual thing. It is not necessarily something material or earthly. It can never be wrong to want Jesus to add to our spiritual well-being.

(iii) Jesus was a person who talked much about reward, and it is not possible to be more spiritual than him. The first step is to free ourselves from preoccupation with praise from each other, and fix our eyes on our Father.

17. Learning to Pray
(Matthew 6:5-8)

Jesus has stated a principle. 'Take care not to perform your righteousness in front of men and women, in order to be seen by them.' He has mentioned one example: our giving to the needy should not be for self-display (6:2-4). Now he mentions another example: our praying should not be for the purposes of self-display either (6:5-15).

It is not surprising that Jesus' second example (6:5-15) should be longer than the other two combined (6:1-4, 16-18). It reflects the great importance of prayer. Matthew's Gospel does not emphasize prayer as much as Luke's Gospel does, but it is still clear that Jesus took prayer seriously.

1. Jesus was man of prayer. It is obvious that Jesus was often to be found praying. We find him telling God of his gratitude (Matt. 11:25-26) or giving thanks for food (Matt. 14:19; 26:26, 27; Mark 6:41; 14:22, 23). On one occasion he spends the best part of a day praying in a lonely place (Matt. 14:23; Mark 6:46; see also Mark 1:35). The occasion when Jesus was transformed in appearance before his disciples took place at a time when Jesus had turned aside for a few days of sustained prayer (Matt. 17:1; Mark 9:2). People expected Jesus to pray for them. Children were brought to Jesus in the hope that he would pray for them to be blessed by God (Matt. 19:13).

Jesus was a man of faith. The cursing of the fig-tree was the result of Jesus' faith (Matt. 21:21; Mark 11:22-24).

113

Jesus was a man of worship. He would sing a song of praise when celebrating the passover festival (Matt. 26:30; Mark 14:26). He resisted the devil by quoting the Scripture and insisting that the Father alone should be worshipped (Matt. 4:10). When Jesus knew he was approaching the cross he wanted to pray, and went to Gethsemane to prepare himself by praying. The occasion (Matt. 26:36-46; Mark 14:32-42) reveals much of Jesus' attitude to prayer. He felt the need of prayer himself, wanted others to pray with him, and urged the disciples to pray for themselves. A few hours later, Jesus was praying even as he was hanging on the cross (Matt. 27:46, 50; Mark 15:34, 37).

2. Jesus takes it for granted that his disciples will pray. He says, *And when you pray....* The way he lived encouraged others to pray. In Matthew 15:31 (and Mark 7:37) we find people glorifying God for the many miracles of Jesus. He made the topic of prayer a major ingredient of his teaching. Jesus gives teaching about prayer not only here (6:5-15), where he asks for sincerity (6:5-6) and simplicity (6:7-8), but also in 7:7-11, where he asks for persistence and expectation. He was quite detailed about the matter. He mentioned particular matters for which his disciples should pray. He urged them to pray for labourers in God's work (Matt. 9:37-38) and to pray that the flight from Jerusalem, during a military invasion, should not fall on a sabbath (Matt. 24:20; Mark 13:18). In 6:9-13 he gives a kind of prayer-list. He teaches the need of forgiveness in prayer in 6:12, 14, 15 (compare Matt. 5:22-26; 18:23-35; Mark 11:25), sincerity in prayer (6:5-7) and the need for

unanimity in prayer (Matt. 18:19). He refers occasionally to fasting (see Matt. 4:2; 6:16-18; 9:14). He calls for faith when we pray (Matt. 21:18-22; Mark 11:22-26).

3. Hypocrites pray as well as disciples. Prayer is one of the world's most popular activities. Hypocrites and pagans 'pray' as well as Jesus' disciples. *And when you pray, you must not be like the hypocrites. For they love to stand and pray in the synagogues and on the street corners, so that they may be seen by other people* (6:5a). When the wise men came seeking to 'worship' Jesus, Herod the Great claimed that he wanted to worship Jesus as well (Matt. 2:2, 8)! The devil was interested in worship also; he wanted to be the one who is worshipped (Matt. 4:9)! He was jealous of God! Many people are interested in prayer in one way or another. But of some it must be said: 'in vain do they worship me' (see Matt. 15:8, 9; Mark 7:6-7). Jesus complained of those who 'for a pretence make long prayers' (Mark 12:40; the text in Matt. 23:14 is uncertain). Somewhat different are the people of Jerusalem – especially the children – who virtually worshipped Jesus at his final entry into the city (Matt. 21:9, 15; Mark 11:9). They could not have much understood what they were doing, but Jesus commended them.

All sorts of people 'love to ... pray', even hypocrites. So loving prayer is not in itself a sign of spirituality! It all depends what sort of praying is involved.

Since prayer has such a good reputation people like to pretend to be more prayerful than they are! If prayer did not have such a good reputation no one would feel the need to indulge in this sort of spiritual fraud. No one should be in the slightest bit interested in getting a phoney and fraudulent reputation for spirituality. Of such people Jesus says, *Truly I say to you, they have their reward* (6:5b). They get what they want – a good reputation. But then that is the end of the matter. No other spiritual blessing will come through their praying. Their reputation for piety is their *only* reward.

4. Jesus asks for privacy in prayer rather than ostentation. The same principle of privacy that applies to giving to the needy also applies to prayer. Of course, Jesus is not condemning public prayer meetings. But he is asking us to shun self-advertizing in connection with prayer. We should go out of our way not to present a picture of ourselves as great pray-ers. I personally wonder whether we ought to announce that certain people are 'intercessors' – although some good friends of mine do it! There is no office of 'intercessor' in the New Testament, and to publicly label a person an 'intercessor' possibly does them damage (I notice that at times they start acting as though they are special leaders of the church and have a superior knowledge of God's will; and they sometimes make bizarre announcements). True intercessors surely will not want such advertizing, and might even want to avoid a publicly acclaimed group of 'intercessors'. They will think it to be a piece of trumpet-blowing. I am sure some Christians have a special ministry of intercession, but I doubt whether any true intercessor wants his or her secret prayerfulness to be announced, whether by trumpet or church secretary.

Do not be like the hypocrites, says Jesus. *But you – when you pray, go into your private room and after you*

*have shut the door pray to your Father in secret, and your
Father who see what happens in secret will reward you*
(6:6). Jesus is using picture language. The vast majority
of the human race do not have a 'private room'. Most
people in the world live two or three to a room at least.
But even in the worst over-crowding it is possible to 'go
into your private room' and 'shut the door'. Jesus did not
have any house that he owned. Yet he would go 'to a lonely
place' (Mark 1:35) or into the hills (Mark 6:46) or would
pray at night when others were asleep.

5. Jesus asks for simplicity in prayer rather than verbosity
or complexity. Some use prayer to draw attention to
themselves. Others have the idea that God is impressed
with the quantity of our praying. *And when you pray, do
not heap up empty words, as the Gentiles do. For they
imagine that they will be heard because of the quantity of
their talk!* (6:7). God does not need us to pour out a flood
of words. He is not impressed by the amount of words we
use, nor by the noise we make, nor by how fluent we are.
Actually God does not need prayer at all! It is *we* who
need prayer, not God. God has ordained that we have our
various needs met and his kingdom goes forward as we
pray. But this is not because he needs to be informed, and
it is not because he needs an outpouring of words. *So you
are not to be like them, says Jesus. For your Father knows
what you need before you ask anything from him* (6:8).
God is not ignorant or reluctant. He does not need our
prayers to inform him or persuade him. But *we* need to
face what it is we want God to do for his kingdom and for
our needs. *We* need the personal contact. God has not

ordained prayer for his own sake; he has ordained it for our sake.

So our praying should be steady and disciplined and thorough. But we do not need to impress others. The more we keep our private praying somewhat hidden from the world – without going to crazy extremes – the better. Of course there are other kinds of praying besides private praying but the word 'you' here is singular. Jesus is referring to individual praying. We learn to pray in simplicity. We pray about lots of things and it is likely to take some time. But we are not to try to keep going in prayer for as long as we can, just for the sake of clocking up some hours. That kind of praying is a bondage! The real secret is to know that God knows all about our desires for his kingdom and needs, and he is more than willing to meet our requests. He has simply ordained that his blessings, which are already lined up for us, come piece at a time as we pray.

18. Praying for God's Kingdom
(Matthew 6:9-10)

Jesus does not leave his teaching about prayer purely in the realm of principles. He gives a prayer-guide: 'the Lord's Prayer' (as it is generally called). It is a list of the topics that should come in our prayers. We do not have to recite it in prayer, although if we do we know that we have covered the main things we ought to pray for! It is for all Christians at all times, and can be easily memorized. If we know the Lord's Prayer by heart, we have a 'prayer list' that is always with us.

It falls into three sections. First the person praying addresses himself to God: *So pray in this way: Our Father who is in heaven, ...* (6:9a). Then the prayer has three petitions which concern God: *may your name be hallowed* (6:9b). *Let your kingdom come. Let your will come to pass* (6:10). Then it has three petitions which concern ourselves: *Give to us today bread sufficient for tomorrow* (6:11), *and forgive us our debts as we have forgiven our debtors* (6:12), *and do not bring us into temptation but rescue us from the evil one* (6:13).

There were plural words in verse 5: 'When *you* (plural) pray ...'. And there were singular words in verses 6-8: 'But when *you* (singular) pray, enter into your private room ...'. Now there are plural words again in verses 9-12: *'Our* Father ... Give *us* today ...'. Verses 6-8 dealt with private prayer, but the language of verses 9-12 is the language of those who are conscious that they are part of God's people everywhere. Although they may be praying alone, they are still aware of the fellowship of God's people and they are praying as one of them.

1. This model prayer invites us to be concerned about the 'approach' to prayer. The prayer begins. *So pray in this way: Our Father who is in heaven, ...* (6:9a). It is not that we have to cringe or grovel on the floor before God. Jesus is not talking about protocol. God is 'Our Father'. This is the great thing that we keep in mind as we pray. Because he is our Father he wants to receive us. The great difficulty many of us have in prayer is that we feel so ashamed or guilty of what we are and what we have done that we feel we cannot approach God. But God is our Father and he

119

wants contact with his children. he wants to hear from us more than we wish to speak to him. We are slandering his fatherhood if we stay away from him through fear or shame.

Because God is our Father he wants to give us more of the Holy Spirit. ('Because you are *sons* God has given us the Spirit of his Son ...'). Because God is our Father he wants to protect us, provide for us and give us a part to play in his kingdom. The prayers of the Bible generally have this sense of depending on God's greatness.

2. Secondly, this model prayer invites us to be more concerned about God's kingdom than about our own necessities. This is a very important matter. Many Christians are very preoccupied with their own personal needs. They worry about salary and finances, paying the rent or (in many parts of the world) school fees. They are concerned about their health, education for their children, comfort, holidays, friendship with the opposite sex, owning their own home, their marriage, helping their extended family, and perhaps the prosperity of their business or their promotion at work or their finding employment.

But the Lord's Prayer invites us temporarily to forget all of these things and concentrate first on God. God has some things he wants just as we have some things that we want. And God wants us to want his will before we want our will. He wants us to attend to the affairs of his kingdom before we attend to the affairs of our little kingdom. This affects our prayers. We begin with our Father and his name, his kingdom and his will. Only then do we come to our own concerns. Because God is our Father we need not be in such a hurry to get to our own needs. He knows all about us and is ready to provide for us.

3. So this model prayer invites us to pray about God's name, God's kingdom and God's will. *May your name be hallowed. Let your kingdom come. Let your will come to pass.* The three petitions almost say the same thing three times over. When God's will is done, that is the coming of God's kingdom, and it is the way in which God gets his name to be sanctified.

God's name is what he is. It is his revealed character, his reputation among men and women when it corresponds to what he really is. Our deepest desires, and the top priority in our praying, should be that men and women get to know God as he really is.

When we pray for the sanctifying of God's name, we are praying for a world where large numbers of people will get to know God as he really is. 'Let those who love your name rejoice in you,' said the psalmist (Ps. 5:11). God wants people to know him by name, by the character that is truly his. This was the reason why Jesus came into the world. 'I have shown your name to the people you gave me,' said Jesus (John 17:6). Now Jesus' disciples continue the work of showing God's name to everyone everywhere. 'Give to God the glory due to his name' (Ps. 96:8). This is something that God greatly wants throughout the world.

We pray for God's kingdom to overcome the world. We want God's kingdom to spread extensively. We ask that every nation might be reached by God's good news of his kingdom. We ask God to bring 'the fulness of the

Gentiles' (Rom. 11:25), just as Jesus prayed for those who would believe in him in future ages (see John 17:20). We are praying that nations might be affected by the presence of large numbers of Christians. We are praying for the day when Israel will be saved and there will be worldwide spiritual awakening as a result. We are praying for God's programme of spiritually conquering the world to be advanced, so that the day when Jesus comes back to this world may be hastened.

If we live and pray as we should, we actually 'hasten' the Day of God. We are asked to believe that in some way we affect how soon the coming of Jesus will be. Praying and living aright actually speeds the coming of the final phase of the kingdom of God. God has promised 'a new heavens and a new earth in which righteousness has its dwelling-place'. Those who live for God will enjoy a new home altogether. A new world is coming. It will quite literally be 'heaven on earth'. Heaven will become earthly; the new Jerusalem will come down on to the earth. We shall dwell with God. There will be no more tears, no more sorrows, no more quarrels, no misunderstanding, no rivalry, no sin, no devil, no tiredness, no poverty, no disease, no death – but only Jesus and the newness of life which goes on for ever. Yet it comes by our praying.

God's will being done is almost the same idea as his kingdom coming. But one term concentrates on what God does when he acts as king; the other concentrates on what men and women do when they carry out God's will. 'Kingdom' focuses on extent, since the kingdom is destined to spread over the globe. But 'will' focuses on intensity or depth. In each place what God wants is to be thoroughly done and fully carried out.

When we pray for what God wants to come about, we are acknowledging that something miraculous is needed in our world, for when man is left to himself God's will is not done. The 'natural man' rebels against God, complains against God, and resents God's wishes. It takes great changes in the hearts of men and women for them to truly want what God wants. 'Incline my heart to your testimonies,' the psalmist prayed (Ps. 119:36). When we pray for God's will to be done, we are praying that God will achieve what he wants in his world. And what he wants is that we should want what he wants. That we should say 'Let what God wants be done'. We are looking to the very end of God's plan when we use the words 'as it is done in heaven', for heaven is a place where God's wishes are fulfilled totally. We are looking for the world to move in the direction of radical and massive change under the impact of the gospel of Jesus, when we pray, 'Your will be done on earth, as it is done in heaven.'

4. This prayer invites us to be ready to be the answer to our own prayers. This prayer is a commitment to a lifestyle. This is part of the reason why we are to pray. It is not that God needs this prayer; we need it. When we pray we are at the same time tuning ourselves and adjusting ourselves to be and to prepare for what we are praying.

This prayer is a commitment to a life of involvement in the worldwide church of the Lord Jesus Christ. How can one pray for God's kingdom to come, if one shows no interest in the wider world. The Lord's Prayer only gives us the headings. Major steps forward in the progress of

God's kingdom come as we pray. But how can we pray if there is no interest, no involvement, in the wider world. We may not be able to travel everywhere. The fashion of prayer-tourism is only for the wealthy! But our prayers can reach places where no tourist can visit. Christian praying does not have a narrow focus. We should be interested in the progress of the gospel everywhere. We travel the world from our little home, not in the luxury of a jumbo jet, but on the wings of prayer.

19. Bread – The Past – The Future
(Matthew 6:11-13)

Having prayed for God's name, God's kingdom, God's will, we are now ready to pray for ourselves. This is a very significant order. It is submissive order. We are submitting ourselves to God and putting his honour and glory before our own. It is a trusting sequence of praying. Often we are panicky about our own needs and want to rush to God for what we are alarmed about, but in the Lord's 'prayer-list' we leave them with God for a time, while we turn to something more urgent, the needs of God's kingdom.

But there is another reason for this order of praying. We are the ones through whom God's name is sanctified, God's kingdom comes, and God's will gets done. Having prayed for God's will to be done, we are now praying about the instruments and tools through whom God's will gets done. Matthew 6:8-10 spoke of ends; Matthew 6:11-13 speaks of the means to the end. There is a kind of logic in the movement from the first three to the second three petitions. All of the six petitions focus on the here-and-now, but the first three also extend out into the future. They are somewhat 'eschatological' (focusing on the future, and looking for the end of the world which might be sooner than we think). We pray in the light of our expectation that God's name will be honoured, that his kingdom will come, that he will receive universal obedience one day. But the second three requests are much more focused on the present. They are what is needed in order to fulfil the purposes of God's kingdom.

The well-known ending to this prayer ('For yours is the kingdom and the power and the glory forever. Amen') was not part of what Jesus said. It was added in the second century when written prayers began to be used in church worship. The best modern translations do not have it.

1. The instruments of God's kingdom need God's material provision. It may seem very earthly and commercial to pray for such a lowly thing as 'daily bread', but that is what we do. We pray: *Give to us today bread sufficient for tomorrow* (6:11). The phrase 'sufficient for tomorrow' (Greek, *epiousios*) has been much discussed by New Testament scholars. It seems to mean 'for the coming day'. As always Jesus is speaking in a very picturesque manner. It is as if someone is praying at night that they will have enough to live on the next day! Many of us plan and pray for 'monthly bread' or 'annual bread' rather than 'daily bread', but Jesus only guarantees 'daily bread'.

It may also seem strange that daily bread is put first of the three, above even the forgiveness of our sins and protection from Satan. But the order is a practical order. The first practical requirement in the instruments of God's kingdom is that they stay alive and well. In this sense, daily bread is their *first* requirement.

How much 'daily bread' should we pray for? May we pray (or even 'claim') to be rich? The order of requests helps us to answer this question. There is a calling of God upon our lives, and there is a will of God for his kingdom. We are praying for the instruments of the kingdom – ourselves, the members of God's worldwide church. We shall be provided for according to the calling of God upon our lives! Some Christians will need to be richer than others in order to achieve their calling and ministry. Others will need to be not so abundantly provided for. Some would be better equipped for ministry if they were poorer! Wealth damages them. One thing is sure. Our daily bread will be enough to keep us alive and well, and it will be enough for us to fulfil God's purposes and plans in our serving him. And it may be added: God is not stingy. He sometimes enjoys giving us basketfuls of leftovers (see Matt. 15:37).

There is no need to think that praying 'Give us bread for tomorrow' stands in contradiction to not being anxious about tomorrow. On the contrary. Praying about tomorrow is the *means* by which we come to freedom from anxiety about tomorrow. I am not anxious about tomorrow *because* I have prayed today about tomorrow!

2. The instruments of God's kingdom have to have the past cleansed. The prayer continues: *and forgive us our debts as we have forgiven our debtors* (6:12).

There are various ways in the Bible in which sin is

regarded. It is 'missing the mark' (Hebrew, *chet'*; Greek, *hamartia);* it is 'wickedness' (Hebrew, *ra'*) and 'rebelliousness' (Hebrew, *pesha'*). It is 'transgression' (Greek, *parabasis*, crossing a line which we are forbidden to cross). It is failure (Greek, *paraptoma)* and lawlessness (Greek, *anomia).* But it is also 'debt' (Greek *opheilemata*). It is an obligation to give to God what is his, but an obligation which we have failed to provide so that we are now in debt to him.

Jesus asks us to admit our sins, and to ask forgiveness for them. It must be remembered that 'forgiveness' has to do with our conscious relationship towards God. It is not the same as Paul's term 'justification'. 'Justification' is outside of us. It is our status as a righteous person in the eyes of God. We do not have to pray each day for 'justification', in Paul's sense of the word. But 'forgiveness' is not just a legal decision in the heart of God. It is God's communicating to us that he is not holding anything against us because of our sins. It is the restoration of a good relationship between us and God. It is the consciousness that God is not angry with us. Forgiveness is a spiritual 'experience'; justification is not. Forgiveness takes place in our hearts; 'justification' takes place in the courts of heaven. Forgiveness has to be daily experienced; 'justification by faith' takes place once in a lifetime and cannot be repeated.

To be forgiven is as necessary as to have one's daily bread. Forgiveness relates to our past. We need to have our past cleansed from guilt. Our usefulness to God and our joy in life is seriously damaged if we are feeling guilty. Guilt has all sorts of horrid side-effects. Relationships with others are spoiled. Prayer is made cold and dry and lifeless. One's appearance and health deteriorates. There are people who will pray for daily bread but not give much thought to the cleansing away of guilt. But one is as necessary as the other.

The Lord's Prayer is a prayer about the kingdom of God. It is really all one single prayer for the progress of his kingdom. Even when we pray for ourselves and for each other (for it is 'our' sins, not 'my sins' that Jesus mentions) we are praying for the equipping of the agents of God's kingdom. Forgiveness and freedom from guilt are vital for the people of God. Their being forgiven is itself part of the progress of the kingdom.

We pray: 'forgive us our debts as we have forgiven our debtors' (6:12). Forgiveness is needed from us towards others, as well as from God towards us. Again we note that Jesus speaks of 'us ... our'. The prayer takes it for granted that the entire people of God are a forgiving people. It does not say 'Forgive us ... *because* we have forgiven our debtors'. It is not that we are *earning* our forgiveness by forgiving others. But we expect to enjoy the spiritual experience of forgiveness in the same way and to the same extent that we allow others to enjoy our forgiveness.

3. The instruments of God's kingdom have to have the future protected. The prayer continues: *and do not bring us into temptation but rescue us from the evil one* (6:13). If the previous clause looked backwards, this clause looks forward. We need cleansing from the past but we are now looking to the future. We shall be tempted again and 'the evil one', Satan, is always near, ready to deceive us. The

word here means both 'tempt' and 'test'. This is a verse where an 'amplified translation' is needed: 'do not bring us into temptation or testing.'

We ask that we shall not be brought *into* temptation. The prayer makes sense if we emphasize the word 'into'. We are not praying that we shall not be tempted – because we know we shall. We are not praying that we shall not be tested – because we know we shall. Something more is meant than simply being tempted, because we shall be tempted every day. Rather we are praying that we shall not be prematurely tested by being brought *into* something that is beyond our strength. The prayer says something about the person praying. It says that we shall not ourselves walk into a situation which is overpowering in its forceful pressure upon us that we should sin. Paul speaks of 'falling' into temptation (1 Tim. 6:9). 'Temptations must come' (Luke 17:1) but we pray that nothing will bring us into them prematurely and unnecessarily. 'Pray that you do not enter *into* temptation,' said Jesus (Matt. 26:41). There is a difference between being tempted and coming *into* temptation so that we are overpowered by it. The remedy to being overpowered in a testing situation is prayer.

We pray to be delivered from the evil one. The one who wants us to sin in times of testing is Satan. God tests; Satan tempts. One remedy is to pray.

We need to pray! It is good to set aside some time regularly. Some time every day (an hour?), some time every week (a morning, an evening?), some time every year (part of a holiday season? the beginning of the year? when the rest of the family is away? For me, the Kenyan cool season when I am away from home is the time for seeking the Lord more energetically, and then my year gets busy again in September.

Our praying must be on a large-scale. We are really praying for one gigantic thing: the coming of God's kingdom. All our prayers are little bits of the great prayer: your kingdom come!

20. Praying for Forgiveness (Matthew 6:14-15)

One part of the Lord's Prayer is worthy of special comment and Jesus goes back to it. *For if you forgive people their trespasses, your heavenly Father will also forgive you* (6:14), *but if you do not forgive other people their trespasses neither will your Father forgive you your trespasses* (6:15).

1. We all need to experience forgiveness. There is no one in this world who does not need to be forgiven by God and by his fellow men and women. None of us can be proud or superior, feeling that others need forgiveness but not we ourselves. This has to be a main topic on our 'prayer list', the Lord's Prayer.

2. We need to remember what 'forgiveness' is. It is a spiritual experience, in which we know that God or the other person is holding nothing against us. It is experiencing God's voice when he lets us know that he has no plans to hold against us what we have done or said.

3. Forgiveness is something that has to be re-experienced regularly. Jesus is not speaking of our coming to our first salvation. Even disciples have to pray, 'Forgive us our debts.' We cannot simply take forgiveness for granted or say 'I was forgiven all my sins past, present and future when I got saved'. There is a sense in which that is true. We were 'justified' when we first trusted Jesus. We were transferred into God's kingdom. There will never be any condemnation for us (as Romans 8:1 says). But forgiveness is a spiritual *experience*; it is not simply an objective fact that happened to us once-and-forever at our conversion. There are some things that happened once-and-for-ever at our conversion but this is not one of them. This is implied in the Lord's Prayer. Why should this petition be in the Lord's Prayer if we did not need to use it? Forgiveness is something experiential and conscious. We need to seek forgiveness from God regularly.

God forgives us at our first conversion. But this is not the end of the matter. We shall need fresh experience of forgiveness almost every day of our lives. Justification is once-for-ever. Forgiveness is freshly sought from God every day. We pray daily, 'Forgive us our debts ...' We never need to pray, 'Lord please justify us today ...' – although I suppose we might pray that way if we were unconverted people believing on Jesus for the first time.

4. What is needed for our sins to be forgiven? Confession, faith – and the forgiveness of others. This last point surprises some people. Is Jesus saying that our salvation comes by our forgiving others? Are we saved by our good works? No, not at all. He does not ask us to pray, 'Forgive

131

us our trespasses *because* we forgive others ...' And he is not dealing with 'justification' or our first receiving salvation. As I have been saying, the Sermon on the Mount is addressed to disciples! What is meant is that the spiritual *experience* of knowing God's forgiveness depends a lot on how we treat others. God gives many promises of forgiveness. The Lord forgives all our sins (see Ps. 103:3). He blots out transgression (Isa. 43:25). But we shall not experience the richness of his forgiveness unless we are forgiving in our attitudes, words and actions towards others.

Also, we shall not be forgiven if we do not confess our sins. The Lord's Prayer implies that we are admitting to God what we have done. 'Forgive us our debts' is just the note in the prayer list. It is just a heading. It implies that we admit to God what we need forgiveness for.

5. We are duty-bound, whether we like it or not, to forgive all our enemies. We must be like Esau, who was badly treated by Jacob but came to the point where he totally forgave him and threw his arms around him (Gen. 33:4). Luther reckoned that in his later years Esau experienced salvation; I reckon Genesis 33:4 is proof that he is right.

We must be like Joseph who forgave his brothers after they had sold him into slavery. It had caused Joseph such suffering, yet Joseph utterly and totally forgave his brothers. 'Do not be distressed,' he said to them. 'Do not be angry with yourselves' (Gen. 45:5). 'It was not you ... but God' (Gen. 45:8) he said, putting things in such a way that allowed them to forgive themselves. 'I will provide for you' (Gen. 45:11). He kissed all his brothers and wept over them (Gen. 45:15).

We must be like David who forgave Saul (1 Sam. 24:8-12; 26:21-25), like Stephen who forgave those who stoned him (Acts 7:60), like Paul who forgave those who opposed him (2 Tim. 4:16). We shall only experience forgiveness to the extent that we forgive others.

Above all, we must be like Jesus who prayed for the forgiveness of his enemies, even as he was being crucified. More than that, Jesus' entire ministry, when in this world and now in heaven, is designed to bring us forgiveness. His blood was shed for our forgiveness. His blood was sprinkled in the heavenly sanctuary and thus presented to the Father – for our forgiveness, His heavenly intercession taking place right now is designed to secure our forgiveness. 'Christ comes forward as intermediary, to change the throne of dreadful glory into the throne of grace.'[25]

But we must give out forgiveness as well as want forgiveness for ourselves. In this matter, what we give is what we get. When we let others know we hold nothing against them, God lets us know that he is holding nothing against us. Forgiveness comes through the cross of Jesus Christ. As in Old Testament sacrifices, 'the priest will make atonement and they will be forgiven' (Lev. 4:20). But the *experience* of forgiveness very much depends on how we treat other people. It is a straightforward command of Jesus (see also Matt. 18:21-35; Luke 7:3-4). We may have to forgive the same person seven times a day (Luke 17:3-4)! But it has got to be done, if we are to continue to experience the presence of God in our lives.

---

25. *Calvin: Institutes of the Christian Religion*, 3:20:17 (translation by F.L. Battles, Westminster Press, 1960).

How much will God forgive us? Well, forgiveness is conditional. Nothing is forgiven if we do not believe in Jesus. But all manner of sins and wickedness will be forgiven, if we put our trust in the atoning blood of Jesus Christ – and then forgive everyone anywhere, people around us, people we lost contact with long ago, everyone everywhere who has ill-treated us. It is very liberating. It brings down upon our lives a rich sense of the love of God.

The key word in Matthew 6:12 is 'as'. 'Forgive us our debts *as* we have forgiven our debtors.' You are forgiven 'as' you forgive. Make the other person feel forgiven; God will make you feel forgiven. Make it easy for the other person to forgive himself; God will make it easy for you to forgive yourself. Make the other person feel that everything has turned out for good. God will make you feel that everything has turned out for good. In this matter, you get what you give.

21. Fasting
(Matthew 6:16-18)

We remember that Matthew 6:1-18 has a general principle (6:1), followed by three examples: giving (6:2-4), prayer (6:5-15)) and fasting (6:16-18).

1. Jesus does not make too much of fasting. In fact, there is not much fuss made in the Bible about fasting.

When you fast, do not look gloomy as the hypocrites do, for they put on a dismal face to show people they are fasting. I tell you the truth, they have their reward in full (6:16). But when you fast, put perfume on your head and wash your face (6:17), so that your fasting may not be noticed by other people, but by your Father who sees in secret; and your Father, who sees what is done in secret, will reward you (6:18).

When the monastic movement started, fasting was given much more prominence in the church. Early scribes copying out New Testament manuscripts tended to add references to fasting which were not in the original manuscripts. Mention of fasting in several New Testament passages is found in later hand-copied texts of the Greek New Testament but are not to be found in the earlier manuscripts. The most well-known four examples are Matthew 17:21 (which is not original in Matthew's Gospel but is taken from Mark 9:29); Mark 9:29 (where the original text has 'This kind does not go out except by prayer'; the words 'and fasting' were added later on in the history of the church); Acts 10:30 (where 'fasting and praying' are found in some inferior manuscripts but are not original); and 1 Corinthians 7:5 (where later manuscripts added 'and fasting' but again the words are not original). In these cases a translation of the *late* manuscripts is found in the Authorised Version, but more accurate modern translations rightly omit the late insertions to the text.

2. Fasting can be done for foolish reasons. 'Religious' people like to fast. Sometimes people like to 'look gloomy ... to show people they are fasting'. The boastful Pharisee of Luke 18 said 'I fast twice a week!' (verse 12). It

somehow makes religious people feel good to go through the slight discomfort of experiencing a little hunger-strike. King Saul put his men on a compulsory fast, demanding that they go without food. But it is foolish to make soldiers go without food, and Jonathan commented on the foolishness of his father (1 Sam. 14:24-30). Queen Jezebel once proclaimed a fast for her own wicked purposes (1 Kgs. 21:9, 12). The enemies of Paul took an oath not to eat or drink until they had killed him – an oath which they must have broken (Acts 23:12-22).

Isaiah 58 is the most important passage about fasting in the Old Testament. Fasting is a time when one is eager to seek God (58:2), yet it is of no value unless other aspects of one's life are pleasing to God. It may be noticed that Isaiah 58:5 speaks of 'a day'. It seems to be a one-day fast that is referred to. The message of the chapter is that prayer is more likely to be heard when one's life is right than when one is fasting and expecting the fasting itself to do some good. Fasting is worthless if other aspects of one's life are not right (see Jer. 14:12).

3. But it is still true that Jesus expected his disciples to fast (see also Matt. 9:15; Mark 2:20; Luke 5:35). We should fast mainly when it is natural to do so. Fasting is largely a matter of common sense and all sorts of people fast for all sorts of reasons, good and bad. It is normally suitable when one is so busy doing something that eating food would be a nuisance, or when one is so overwhelmed with sorrow that one does not feel like eating. Moses did not take food with him when he went up Mount Sinai. On a later occasion when the people of Israel were defeated

in battle they prayed for a day and it was not suitable for
them to be cooking meals (Judg. 20:26). Hannah did not
feel like eating when she was praying for a child (1 Sam.
1:7, 8). There was a one day fast at Mizpah at a time of
national confession of sin (1 Sam. 7:6). Having meals at
such a time would be inappropriate. Jonathan was so
distressed at his father's behaviour that for a day he wanted
no food (1 Sam. 20:34). A prophet was told to fast during
one particular task that God had for him to do (1 Kgs.
13:8-24). Ahab once went without food because he was
distressed at God's word of judgment against him (1 Kgs.
21:27). The crowds following Jesus went without food in
order to be with Jesus (Matt. 15:32; Mark 8:3). Paul went
without food when God struck him blind (Acts 9:9).

Sometimes the leaders of God's people might call for a
fast-day. Nehemiah called for a one-day fast for the
purpose of giving time to God (Neh. 9:1). Jeremiah speaks
of 'a day' of fasting (Jer. 36:6, 9). The early church fasted
when it was seeking to commence a new work for God
(Acts 13:2, 3), and when appointing elders (Acts 14:23).
Daniel fasted when seeking the fulfilment of God's promises
to Israel (Dan. 9:1-3). Joel called for a fast because locusts
were invading Israel (Joel 1:14; see also 2:15). The people
of Nineveh did something similar (Jon. 3:5-9).

4. Fasting should be undertaken when it is natural to do
so. Sometimes fasting is a very *natural* thing to do. In
certain times of life a person may be 'with constant distress
in his bones, so that his very being finds food repulsive
and his soul loathes the choicest meal' (as Job 33:19-20
puts it). Times of bereavement, times when one greatly

137

feels the need for prayer, times of confession, times of
emergency – these are times for fasting. All of the mentions
of fasting in the Bible are on such occasions. David gave
himself to prayer and fasting when his 'prayers were
returned unanswered' (Ps. 35:13) or when he faced
persecution (Ps. 69:10). When one is seeking God
energetically fasting is natural (see Joel 2:12). Sometimes
one fasts without even noticing that one is doing so. Jesus
got so busy talking to the woman of Samaria that he went
without food and lost all sense of hunger. His disciples
thought someone had given him food (John 4:31-34). In
distressing times one's tears are one's food (see Ps. 42:3).
'I *forget* to eat my food,' said the psalmist of Psalm 102:4.
Even foolish people may 'loathe all food' in times of
extreme distress (Ps. 107:17, 18). King Darius could
neither eat nor sleep after he had put Daniel in a den of
lions (Dan. 6:18).

The day of atonement required that everyone 'humble
their souls' during that day (Lev. 16:29, 31; 23:27, 32;
Num. 29:7). This was taken to involve fasting (see Acts
27:9 which refers to the day of atonement).

Some people are called to fast more than others. Anna
in Luke 2:37 obviously had a special ministry of prayer
and fasting. So did John the Baptist (Matt. 11:18; Luke
7:33).

The majority of references to fasting show us that
normally fasting is for *one* day or 'until the sun sets' (2
Sam. 1:12; 3:35). When a matter is very serious it might
be for *three* days. Nehemiah fasted 'for some days' (Neh.
1:4) when he heard distressing news. In the days of Esther
the Israelites did the same when they heard distressing

news (Est. 4:3). Later Esther requested a three-day fast in preparation for her going to see the Persian king. A major crisis once led David to fast for *seven* days. He was so distressed that for seven days he did not want to eat (2 Sam. 12:16-23). Fasting may be a part of mourning in which case it might be for seven days (1 Sam. 31:13; 1 Chron. 10:12).

Daniel once went on a partial fast (using only light food) for *three weeks* (Dan. 10:2, 3). If one wants to go on a lengthy time of prayer and fasting, this is often the best way to do it. A much more heavy fast – and one which should not be followed without exceptional guidance – is the forty-day total fast without food or water. Jesus fasted for forty days (Matt. 4:2; Luke 4:2). Moses fasted this way on Mount Sinai (Exod. 34:28; Deut. 9:9, 18). Elijah once travelled for forty days without food (1 Kgs. 19:8). Such a fast requires supernatural strength. Normally it cannot be done (because the body cannot go such a length of time without water). In the three cases known to us (Jesus, Moses, Elijah), there is reason to think each had the help of angels. So far as we know Jesus only did this once in his lifetime.

There are times when it is inappropriate to fast. After a time of prayer had finished, David said, 'Why should I fast?' (2 Sam. 12:23). The time for fasting was finished. In the days of Zechariah, the question was asked whether traditional days of fasting should continue (Zech. 7:3-5); they were changed into days of feasting (Zech. 8:19)! It was not a time for fasting when Jesus was with the disciples and they were rejoicing in having him with them (Matt. 9:14-15; Mark 2:18-20; Luke 5:33-35).

We should fast when we need specially to seek God in prayer. Jehoshaphat asked Judah to fast and seek God at a time when the nation was in danger (2 Chron. 20:3). Ezra proclaimed a fast when he asked those travelling with him to seek protection for their journey (Ezra 8:21-23). He spent a day fasting when he discovered the people of Judah were in danger of going back to idolatry (Ezra 9:1, 5) or were showing faithlessness towards God (Ezra 10:6). These biblical examples encourage us to fast, but it should be a natural thing, led by the Holy Spirit and suiting the occasion. We fast when eating and preparing food would be a nuisance and a hindrance to spiritual activities.

5. Jesus' main point is that we fast in a natural manner. Jesus' disciples are to behave in an entirely natural manner when they fast. They fast to God alone. Our Father, who sees secret prayerfulness will reward them.[26]

---

26. I quote all the main passages of the Bible concerning fasting. Some other passages might be quoted but are not really relevant, such as Genesis 24:33; Leviticus 23:14; Numbers 6:3, 4; 1 Samuel 30:11, 12. Saul's day of fasting before he died was not a sign of spirituality; he simply did not feel like eating (1 Sam. 28:20); 2 Samuel 11:11 does not suggest Uriah was fasting. Ahab once refused food but there was nothing spiritual about it (1 Kgs. 21:4, 5). Daniel's refusal of the king's food was not fasting in the normal sense of the term (Dan. 1:12-16). Acts 27:21, 33 does not really refer to religious fasting. Nor do Romans 14:21; 1 Corinthians 8:13; 2 Corinthians 6:5; 11:27; 1 Timothy 4:3. Esther 9:31 seems to suggest there was a day of fasting in connection with the festival of Purim (see Est. 9:31), but if so it must have been before the feasting which was the main part of the occasion (9:18, 19, 22).

22. Treasure in Heaven
(Matthew 6:19-24)

Jesus moves from intensely spiritual matters, generosity
to the needy (6:2-4), praying (6:5-15) and fasting (6:16-
18), to something much more earthly and ordinary: our
attitude towards money and possessions. The Christian
has to be able to handle these two sides of life: the spiritual
and the ordinary. We have to be able to give to the needy
and pray and fast. But we also need to handle money and
possessions.

Jesus, first of all, gives us a blunt command, negatively
and positively: *Do not lay up for yourselves treasure on
earth...* (6:19a), *but lay up for yourselves treasures in
heaven...* (6:20a). The command cannot totally forbid any
savings or use of capital altogether. 'Moth' (6:19) refers
to clothing and it cannot be sinful to have some spare
clothes. The emphasis is on the word 'treasure'. Riches
and earthly blessings are not to so captivate our interest
and our energy that we look to them as the greatest blessing
in life.

We have already seen that 'reward in heaven' is one of
the major themes of Scripture. Satan claimed to be able to
give earthly rewards to Jesus, but Jesus turned down his
offer (Matt. 4:8-9). The Beatitudes included the offer of
reward. The 'meek shall inherit the earth,' (5:5) said Jesus
– and the word 'inherit' always refers to reward.
Persecution is to be endured because 'your reward in
heaven is great' (5:12). Part of the reward is honour. The
person who fulfils the law, outstripping the righteousness
of the scribes and Pharisees, will be 'called great' in the

kingdom of heaven (5:19). Love that goes beyond the love of ordinary people brings reward, says Jesus (5:46). The supreme reason why our righteousness is a matter of living with our eye on God is that if we live in any other way we lose our reward from our Father who is in heaven (6:1). Generosity (6:2-4), prayerfulness (6:5-15), and sensible fasting (6:16-18) are rewarded. Our Father who sees in secret rewards us (6:4, 6, 18).

The idea that a Christian should *not* live for reward is nonsense. It is true that our basic salvation is not a matter of reward; that is sheer gift 'without works' (Eph. 2:8, 9). But upon the basis of the salvation that is given us, the way we live will be rewarded or penalised. It does matter how we live. Reward is one of the themes of Scripture, and the one who spoke most about it was Jesus. We must not try to be more spiritual than Jesus! Gratitude alone is not a sufficient motive for the Christian life.

Matthew 6:20 now puts all of this in terms of a positive command: *but lay up for yourselves treasures in heaven....* Living for heavenly reward is the opposite of living for earthly reward.

Then Jesus goes on to give us various reasons why we should obey the commands of 6:19a and 20a. There are basically four of them.

1. Earthly treasure is insecure (6:19-20).

Do not lay up for yourselves treasure on earth, where moth and rust consume and where thieves break in and steal (6:19), but lay up for yourselves treasures in heaven, where neither moth nor rust consume anything, and where thieves do not break in and steal (6:20).

It is not worth the trouble accumulating too much earthly treasure, since it cannot be kept. Everything earthly deteriorates. Earthly treasures are transitory. Money devalues. Clothes fade and are ruined by moth and by the passing of time. Cars get stolen. Our personal appearance deteriorates as we get older. One day we will leave this world altogether and will take nothing with us – except our character and our achievements for God. Life is full of worms and rats and mice and moths. Only what is done for Jesus truly lasts for ever. Live too much for this world and you discover how fast things wear out, erode away or get stolen.

But everything that is truly done for God is somehow 'accumulated' in heaven, and nothing in heaven fades or deteriorates. Exactly how treasures are laid up in heaven is not completely revealed to us. It does not yet appear what we shall be (1 John 3:2). It certainly has a lot to do with honour coming from Jesus. It has to do with a level of visible glory, if 1 Corinthians 15:41b-42a is a clue. The reward has to do with God himself. If this is remembered, it answers some difficulties we might have. There is nothing earthly or 'commercial' about heavenly reward. It is said 'The highest reward never comes to him who is seeking it'. That might be true if the reward is something *other* than God himself, but what if the 'highest reward' is God himself taking pleasure in us. Actually, the highest reward *does* come to the one who is seeking it. But the 'highest reward' is surely that God takes pleasure in us, publicly, loudly, eternally.

2. Living for earthly treasure affects your heart. *For where your treasure is, there your heart will be also* (6:21). Whatever we make to be the chief attraction for us in this world has a habit of getting hold of us. It grabs our heart. We think of it, or are thrilled by the prospects of what we shall do or what we shall have. We want to travel here or build this house. We want to prosper in business so as to outclass all rivals. We want our money in the bank to reach a certain level so we can do this or that. The trouble is that such things grasp our attention too much. Such worldly ambitions can even be semi-spiritual. We want our churches to grow to such-and-such a size. We want to become famous in Christian ministry. Even such semi-spiritual ambitions can push God out of our thinking and can become to us worldly treasure. Jesus has already told us that some want the 'treasure' of being famous for generosity, for prayer, for fasting. Maybe they get the fame they want – but lose heavenly reward.

It is a terrible thing when our heart gets gripped by the wrong sort of treasure. There is really only one thing that is worth being 'treasure' to us, and worthy of our day-dreams, worthy of our ambitions, worthy to be excited about – and that is our relationship to God. That is what should capture our hearts. 'All that thrills my soul is Jesus' says the song. That is the way to live. Anything less will bring cynicism, slow deterioration in the things of God – and loss of heavenly reward.

3. Living for earthly treasure damages our ability to see spiritual things clearly.

The lamp of the body is the eye. If therefore your eye is simple, your whole body will be full of light (6:22), but if your eye is evil, your whole body will be darkness. If therefore the light that is within you is darkness, how great is that darkness! (6:23)

Jesus uses an illustration. The eye is the 'lamp' of the body. It enables the body to know where it is going. With good eyesight you walk straight, you see clearly, you avoid accidents. With damaged eyesight, you knock things over, you stumble on uneven ground, you fall down stairs, you bump into obstacles. If what is meant to give you light – the eye – is damaged, you are in bad trouble.

There is a spiritual equivalent. Our 'eye' is our spiritual perceptiveness. Our ambitions are like spiritual eyesight. If we are eager to lay up treasure in heaven, we have good spiritual eyesight. We see clearly the things of God. If we are greedy for earthly treasures, we have damaged eyesight. When we come to see that the real treasure of life is that which we lay up in heaven, that which is done for Jesus, then we are seeing life as it really is. Demas fell in love with this present world, says 2 Timothy 4:10. Perhaps he loved earthly prosperity or a comfortable life or the attractions of worldly pleasures. Whatever it was, he lost his spiritual vision, and could no longer see clearly the surpassing value of a life lived for God.

4. Living for earthly treasure damages and produces an impossible division of loyalty. The last reason not to try to serve God but at the same time live for earthly treasure is that it cannot be done! *No one is able to serve two masters, for either he will hate one and love the other, or*

145

he will hold to one and despise the other. You cannot serve God and mammon (6:24). The picture is of a slave in the ancient world and two slave-owners. It is simply impossible to be the servant of two masters. Both God and 'Mammon' want to be our 'Master'. (Mammon is an Aramaic word meaning 'the idol of wealth'). Of course, one can be the slave of two masters, one after the other. And the slave-girl of Acts 16:16 had more than one master. But one cannot be the servant of two masters who are hostile to each other and have different wishes. God wants us to be his willing, happy slaves! But we cannot be his servants in this way and live for earthly treasures at the same time. One will pull us one way; the other will pull us another way. Their commands will often conflict and we shall have to decide which master we are going to obey. One commands us to walk by faith; the other commands us to walk by sight. One calls us to be humble; the other summons us to a proud way of life. One calls us to seek happiness in himself; the other calls us to seek happiness in things. We cannot serve both. Which one will be our master?

23. Anxiety
(Matthew 6:25-30)

The next matter to be considered is anxiety. One might think that laying up treasure on earth and anxiety are alternatives, as if one person is greedy and eager to lay up treasure in heaven, while the next person is anxious. But they are not alternatives; one can be greedy and anxious

146

at the same time, and greed in fact causes anxiety! Jesus connects the two dangers: *For this reason...* Because we do not want to lay up treasure on earth we are not to be anxious. Anxiety is the result of laying up treasure on earth. Refusal to be anxious about such matters is one way of refusing to lay up treasure on earth.

What needless trouble anxiety gives us! Anxiety in the heart of any person weighs it down. Anxiety chokes the Word of God. Anxiety sets our minds gadding around with all sorts of panicky imaginations, 'when my anxious thoughts multiply within me' (Prov. 12:25; see Mark 4:19; Ps. 94:19).

Once again Jesus begins with a blunt command: *For this reason, I say to you, do not be anxious ... do not be anxious...* (6:25a).

Again Jesus gives various arguments to support his command. There are seven of them which we may pick out.

1. The larger matter is life and the body (6:25b). Jesus says, *For this reason, I say to you, do not be anxious about your life, about what you shall eat or what you shall drink. And do not be anxious about your body, what clothing you shall wear* (6:25a). We are not allowed to be anxious even about the basic necessities of life ('what you shall eat or what you shall drink'), nor about what is needed for us to preserve dignity and self-respect ('what clothing you shall wear'). Jesus asks us to think about the larger matter: *Is not life more than food, and the body more than clothing?* (6:25b). The argument is: if God has done the greater thing, will he not do the lesser thing? If he gave us

147

life, will he now deny us food and drink in order to maintain that life? If he gave us a body, will he deny us clothing to protect and cover that body? If he has done the greatest thing, the giving of soul and body, will he not give the smaller things to keep soul and body alive. (The Greek word for *life* here is *psuche*, soul).

2. If God provides for birds, he will provide for his people. *Consider the birds of the air. Consider that they do not sow seed nor do they gather a harvest or gather things into store-houses, and yet your heavenly Father feeds them. Are you not worth much more than they?* (6:26).

The birds of the air are provided for by God's arrangements. They do not need to indulge in feverish sowing or harvesting or collecting for the future. God arranges the world such that they are provided for in the course of nature.

The previous argument was from the greater to the lesser: If he has done the greatest thing, the giving of soul and body, will he not give the smaller things to keep soul and body alive. Now the argument is from the lesser to the smaller. If he has made arrangements for the smaller creatures of planet earth, will he not also make arrangements for those who are his special people? We have a relationship with God ('your heavenly Father') which the birds do not have. We are of greater value to God than those creatures who are not made in his image.

The whole thrust of Jesus' argument is that we are not to worry very much about these matters at all. Of course we take necessary steps to provide for ourselves. We do sow seed and gather into barns – or banks. But the ultimate source of our provision is God. He can provide for us without sowing or reaping if it is necessary. He does it for the birds of the air. When it is necessary he can do it for us.

It is noticeable in all of this that Jesus is asking us to think. There are many who, if we confessed to being anxious, would want to pray for us or 'cast out the demon of anxiety'. Jesus certainly prayed for his disciples, but here he is ministering to them by teaching them and persuading them to think. If they see the way in which God is their Father, if they see that it is entirely impossible that he should abandon them to be without food or clothing, then they will be delivered from anxiety.

3. Worry achieves nothing. Jesus' next argument is a very plain and ordinary one. *And which of you by being anxious can add a cubit to the length of his life* (6:27). Anxiety is foolish. It accomplishes nothing. It unfits us for life. It weakens our ability to cope with the very thing we are anxious about. It is a form of unbelief. Maybe we worry about how long we shall live. But the worrying does not add a millimetre to how long we shall live. (It is striking that Jesus should use a measure of length and apply it to time, but that is what he does.) It is a very obvious and practical reason for not worrying; worry is entirely useless to achieve anything. The length of our life is entirely in the hands of God. No one can shorten it. No one can lengthen it. The life of simple faith and the taking of ordinary practical common-sense measures will keep us alive and will maintain us in the way of fulfilling our destiny. God is totally in control. The obedient disciple of Jesus need not have the slightest anxiety about these everyday matters.

149

None of this means that in everyday matters we shall never have crises or tragedies. But it does mean that even the crises and the tragedies are in the control of God. Nothing will happen to the obedient Christian that is not in some way within the will and control of God. God may test us and at times even seem to betray us, but persistent faith will bring us through, no matter what happens to us. Worry is to be rejected and refused as a crippling hindrance and as needless unbelief.

Matthew 6:28-30 expands the kind of argument we had in 6:26. It is not a new point but says about flowers something similar to what was previously said about birds.

And why are you so anxious about clothing? Look at how the lilies of the field grow. They do not do any hard labour and they do not make clothes for themselves (6:28). Yet I tell you, not even Solomon in all of his glorious clothing was clothed like one of these (6:29). But if God so clothes the grass of the field, which is there today but tomorrow is thrown into the furnace, will he not much more clothe you, you people with little faith? (6:30)

The clothing of the flowers is provided for by God's arrangements. Again the flowers do not need to indulge in feverish or panicky concern about how they will look! God arranges the world such that they are provided for in the course of nature. If God has made arrangements for temporary passing creatures like the flowers, will he not also make arrangements for those who are his special people? Solomon's glorious clothing was no more beautiful than the beauty of God's creation. Yet we are not to be 'thrown into the furnace' of destruction like dead grass; we are Jesus' disciples and 'the person who does the will of God remains for ever' (1 John 2:17). Surely God *must* provide for us.

It is worth noticing that Jesus has here a 'deliverance ministry'! There is a danger that the disciples will be in the grip of anxiety and Jesus wants to deliver them from it. But his 'deliverance ministry' consists in teaching! He gives them arguments and deductions and logical reasons why there is no need for them to be anxious. Much 'deliverance ministry' today consists only in praying for people. I am sure Jesus prayed for his disciples, but at the same time he gave them many solid arguments for never falling into anxiety again. In his 'deliverance ministry' his praying and his teaching went alongside each other. Anyone who grasps hold of the fact that human beings are greater than the flowers should never be anxious again.

4. Anxiety is a failure of faith. 'Will he not much more clothe you, you people with little faith?' We have to learn to apply our faith on a daily basis. It is all very well for us to say that we are believing God for our eternal salvation. But we have to believe God for our daily needs as well. Christians with 'little faith' are people who have a general faith that God will forgive their sins and bring them to heaven, but who struggle with particular problems that give them anxiety. But Jesus says, 'Apply your faith to these little problems that you are worried about.' The faith that you have in God as a Saviour and Redeemer, put that same faith in God as Protector, Provider, as your Judge amidst injustice, as your closest Friend when all other friends let you down. Go on believing no matter what!

Whatever might be happening to you, believe that God will be with you. I am to be like Esther. I say to myself, 'If I perish, I perish!' – but I am going to go on trusting in my heavenly Father.

> Begone, unbelief! My Saviour is near,
> and for my relief will surely appear.
> By prayer let me wrestle
> and he will perform.
> With Christ in the vessel
> I smile at the storm.

24. Seeking First God's Kingdom (Matthew 6:31-34)

Jesus has given several reasons why his disciples should refuse anxiety. (1) The largest gifts of God are life and the body; God will provide for the smaller thing as he has provided for the larger thing (6:25). (2) If God provides for birds and flowers, he will provide for his people (6:26, 28-30). (3) Worry achieves nothing (6:27). (4) Anxiety is a failure of faith (6:30). Now Jesus has more to say.

5. Worldly concern is characteristic of the Gentiles. *So do not be anxious, saying, 'What shall we eat?' or 'What shall we drink?' or 'What clothes shall we wear? (6:31), for the Gentiles seek all these things ...* (6:32a). It is typical of pagans – ancient and modern – to be endlessly pursuing security in material things, in luxurious food, in ostentatious clothing. The Christian, although there is no

advantage in his being half-starved or dowdy, has his interest entirely elsewhere.

The Christian is meant to be radically and noticeably different from the pagan people, ancient and modern. Talk to any pagans for long and you will find their heart is in money or success in business. They worry about food or boast about what good restaurants they have been in. Or if they are poor and cannot afford such things, they spend their time and their dreams worrying about how to get to be able to afford such things, and so catch up with the wealthier people who enjoy such a life.

So the question that we Christians must ask ourselves is: Are we any different? If we also are worried and anxious about food and clothing and prestige and luxurious holidays and whether we can get sufficient wealth to live an easier life – then we are not different from the paganism we claim to have been rescued from!

No, what we regard as essential to life is entirely different. We scarcely have to bother overmuch with such things as food and clothing. We do what is necessary and sensible but we know our heavenly Father has such things in his care. We are not to be lazy or foolish in such matters, but neither are we to be panicky or anxious. We concentrate on an entirely different realm, the kingdom of God. We find our greatest pleasures in our relationship to God, his love for us, our serving him. Our greatest joys come from our fellowship with his people. Our joys are spiritual joys supremely. What thrills us and moves us is not an increase in salary but progress in the kingdom of God. Jesus wants us to see how radically different we are to be from the average pagan around us. All of this leads to another point.

6. Worldly concern implies distrust of God's knowledge or care. *The Gentiles seek all these things. Your heavenly Father knows that you need them all* (6:32b). It is encouraging to note that Jesus does accept that we need food and clothing and 'all these things'. Jesus tells us not to worry about them, but he is not saying that we have no need of them! We do need them! The Christian is not to look like a gaunt ascetic monk. And there is no need for his clothes to look as though they came from the local jumble sale! 'You need them!' says Jesus. The Christian faith is not worldly, but neither is it so unworldly that it pretends this world does not exist. As if clothing or food were unnecessary!

The point is that our heavenly Father *knows that you need them all!* We take encouragement in God's knowledge and concern. The extent to which we worry has a lot to do with how much we grasp hold of the fact that God knows and cares about us. We know it as a doctrine, perhaps, but it has to be more than a 'doctrine'. It has to be a conviction that grips our heart so that it releases from the slightest anxiety. When we realise that God accepts that we *do* have serious practical needs, when we realise that God knows and cares – then we are released and delivered from anxiety and can give our attention to other things.

All of this leads our Lord Jesus Christ to bring his teaching about earthly treasures and anxieties to two practical commands.

The first concerns our priority. *But seek first the kingdom and his righteousness, and all these things shall be supplied to you in addition* (6:33).

It is a matter of *seeking* something. The blessings of the Christian life do not come by passivity or laziness. God requires that we seek his kingdom diligently. It takes time and effort.

We are to seek his *kingdom*. Jesus is not referring to seeking salvation. The 'kingdom' of God is his royal power at work in our lives. It involves desiring God's presence, desiring to please him so that we experience his approval. It involves taking the time and trouble to forward his kingdom. The beatitudes describe the life of the 'kingdom'. The Lord's prayer told us to pray for the progress of the 'kingdom'. Where the Gentiles seek treasures and pleasures, the Christian seeks to know God and do his will.

We are to seek his *righteousness*. We seek to live the life of godliness. Righteous people are

Assured of God's love,
Bold in testimony,
Courageous when facing threat,
Daring in ventures for God,
Enduring in trial,
Free in the Holy Spirit,
Gracious towards people,
Hopeful in facing the future,
Informed in God's Word,
Joyful in all circumstances,
Kindly towards everyone,
Loving,
Motivated,
Neighbourly,

Obedient,
Patient,
Quick in responding to God,
Regular in spiritual disciplines,
Scriptural in their belief,
Transparent,
Unselfish,
Victorious in spiritual warfare,
Watchful,
e**X**ceptional among the people of the world,
Yearning for God's blessing,
Zealous for God's kingdom.

Righteousness! All-round zeal for pleasing God. There are many who are eager to seek treasures and pleasures. God asks us to seek the progress of his kingdom and the righteousness of his kingdom.

It does not mean only God's righteousness in our own lives, although that is a good place to begin. It also means that we seek to spread around his righteousness in the world. 'Righteousness' is outward-looking and unselfish. It touches society as well as piety.

When we live this way we find that God adds to us 'all these things'. Even some worldly profit might come to us when we are not seeking it at all. It will come partly because God likes to reward us. When we lose our lives, he likes to give them back to us. But 'all these things' are added in other ways. When people see that we are not living for worldly wealth, they begin to trust us with worldly wealth. People like to do business with an unselfish person, and someone not seeking worldly treasure is soon noticed as an unselfish and trustworthy person. Then, in addition, the spiritually minded person does not throw his money away on foolish pleasures. The luxurious life of wine, women and waste is expensive. The godly life of seeking God's kingdom has a tendency to conserve what God gives us. When we seek first God's kingdom we may well find (although it is not a strict rule) that material blessings tend to drift in our direction. Of course, if we seek God's kingdom with this in mind, then we are not seeking God's kingdom!

God's promise is absolute and trustworthy. If we seek his kingdom, our needs will be met.

Jesus' second practical command invites us to take life one day at a time. *So do not be anxious about tomorrow, for tomorrow will worry about itself. Each day's trouble is enough* (6:34). God likes us to deal with the present and he likes us neither to worry about tomorrow or, on the other hand, to fantasize in a self-centred manner over our future successes (see Jas. 4:13-16). The principle is: take one day at a time. Of course some humble planning is encouraged, but neither anxiety nor arrogant self-confidence is allowed.

Jesus talks about 'tomorrow' as if it were a person. Let that person called 'Tomorrow' do his own worrying, Jesus says. 'Tomorrow' comes to us as a kind of demon wanting to seize us and harass us. Lloyd-Jones even says, 'There are cases where this condition is undoubtedly the result of the work of evil spirits.'[27] There can be something weirdly demonic about the way in which 'Tomorrow' comes to assault us and harass us. But don't you worry about him,

---

27. Lloyd-Jones, *Sermon* 2, p.148.

says Jesus. Let him worry about himself!

Nothing can happen without God's permission. We only get feeble and without energy when we allow ourselves to be gripped with anxiety. Do not anticipate the future more than what is reasonably likely. Focus on the knowledge and concern and power of your heavenly Father. He has never abandoned you before; he will not do so ever! Don't go out to meet trouble half-way. If we had to carry a huge bundle of heavy loads all at one time we would be crushed by the weight. But God unties the bundle and gives us one little day's load to bear each day. In this manner we shall find we can carry each day's load quite easily.

So every day has its batch of problems. It is as if they are delivered at our door every day with today's date on them. We take them one batch at a time, and we have to handle them. We forget the past; we don't worry about tomorrow; we do what has to be done today! It is surprising how much we can get done for God when we approach things in that manner. Similarly, we look for the grace of God to arrive in daily packages also! As your days are, so shall your strength be. We find 'grace to help in the time of need', neither sooner nor later. If tomorrow brings a new batch of troubles, there will come in the same post a new parcel of promises, a new provision of God's grace. Refuse anxious thoughts and look for each day to bring sufficient grace for the day.

25. Judging
(Matthew 7:1-6)

In the progress of thought in the Sermon on the Mount, we have moved from the character of the disciple (5:3-16), to the way in which he or she fulfils the Mosaic law (5:17-48) and lives in the sight of God (6:1-18) without laying up treasure on earth (6:19-34).

There are now remaining seven small units of teaching in the Sermon on the Mount. Matthew 7:1-6 forbids a judging attitude towards others. Matthew 7:7-11 invites us to prayer, and 7:12 seems to bring the Sermon on the Mount to a kind of conclusion by giving us a 'golden rule' by which to live. The rest of the sermon consists of exhortations that we should actually live this life which is being set before us. We must enter the kingdom (7:13-14) and beware of the false prophets who would hinder our doing so (7:15-20). There are prophets who seem orthodox but who do not encourage the life of holiness (7:21-23). The wise person will build his 'house' on Jesus and his words (7:24-27). What all this amounts to, then, is this. If Matthew 6:1-18 invites us to live in the sight of God, and Matthew 6:19-34 invites us to live in dependence on God, Matthew 7:1-27 invites us to live in readiness for the judgment of God. The section begins and ends with the theme of God's judgment (7:1-6, 24-27).

Again Jesus follows a similar style to that which we have already seen in 6:1, 19, 25. A blunt command (*Do not judge...,* 7:1a) is followed by the various reasons why we should not have a judgemental attitude.

We are asked not to have a judgemental attitude. *Do*

not judge.... Of course we often have to 'judge' in the sense of 'think', 'consider', 'evaluate' (see 1 Cor. 5:3; 1 John 4:1). The Sermon on the Mount itself asks us to think, and to take note of false prophets. It is not telling us never to express an opinion about others. Jesus himself is the embodiment of the Sermon on the Mount and he certainly shared God's Word boldly concerning many topics and many kinds of people. 'Judge' is being used here in the sense of 'condemn' or 'pass final judgement as if we were God'. We are not to act as if we are God. 'Judgment is mine,' says God (Rom. 12:19). 'Judge nothing before the time,' says Paul. God is the searcher of hearts. He – and he alone – is capable of fully assessing genuineness and integrity. Our opinions are at best provisional. Even when we assess the other person correctly we do not know all the factors that make him what he is or lead him to act as he does. We do not know what has been in his past. We do not know what his physical make-up is. Yet much of our behaviour is physically driven; our sins are 'deeds of the body' (Rom. 8:13). The other person's physical constitution may not be ours and if we were made the way he or she is made we would have the same problems they have. All this must lead us into a non-judgmental approach to other people. We may assess and evaluate what they do and what they say, but we had best be careful of speaking out our assessment of their hearts or their motivation. Sometimes we can see what motivates a person; Solomon could in 1 Kings 3:16-28. But we are not always as skilful as Solomon and even Solomon in 1 Kings 3 was not passing final judgment on anyone. We evaluate (when we have to) what people do and say – but we remember that we are not God and we are not to speak as if we were the final judge of the hearts of men and women. We can look on outward appearance but only the Lord can evaluate the heart.

Jesus goes on to say why we should not have this censorious attitude towards other people.

1. It brings judgment upon ourselves (7:1b-2). *Do not judge, so that you will not be judged* (7:1). *For with the judgment you give others, you will be judged, and the measure you give will be the measure you get* (7:2). It is partly a matter of human response as well. A critical spirit towards others invites criticism back towards ourselves. When we criticize the other person will think to himself – or perhaps say to us – 'But you do this and that...'. The other person takes our judgments and returns them to us! Our remarks make them evaluate us by what we say.

Yet Jesus' words surely mainly refer to God's judgment. Remember the saying about forgiveness in the Lord's prayer – our forgiveness brings God's forgiveness. Matthew 7:1 puts the matter the other way around. Our severity brings upon us God's severity. If we claim to be 'teachers' in our censorious attitudes we get severer judgment from God (see Jas. 3:1). To whom much is given much is required. The expert in moral analysis will be treated as an expert in moral analysis!

2. It is weirdly inconsistent (7:3-4). *And why do you see the speck of dust in the eye of your brother, but in your own eye you do not take note of a plank of wood?* (7:3). We are all perfectionists when we consider other people but extremely tolerant when we look at ourselves!

161

Or how can you say to your brother, 'Let me take out that speck of dust'? Look also at the plank in your own eye! (7:4). It is bad enough that we think this way, but then we proceed to talk to our brother or sister in the Christian fellowship 'Let me take out the speck of dust ...', we say.

3. It damages the disciples' helpfulness to each other. *You hypocrites, first take out the plank of wood from your own eye, and then you will see clearly enough to take out the speck of dust from the eye of your brother* (7:5). It is not that Jesus does not want us to help each other with specks of dust in our eyes. The more we are able to help each other the better! But the question is: who is capable of doing it? A person with real interest in helping others is always someone who is a severe critic of himself. Only one who is a severe critic of himself is really capable of helping anyone else. What is more ridiculous than a man with a plank of wood in his eye trying to be an eye-specialist in the lives of others.

4. It invites an angry response (7:6). '*Do not give to dogs what is holy, and do not throw your pearls before pigs. If you do they will trample them down with their feet and turn to attack you.*' The phraseology is probably chiastic (that is, having an A-B-B-A structure). It can be translated:

    A. Do not give to dogs what is holy,
        B. and do not throw your pearls before pigs.
        B. If you do the pigs will trample down the pearls with
                           their feet
    A. and the dogs will turn to attack you.

It is often said that the Sermon on the Mount consists of random sayings strung together loosely. Actually, there is logical sequence and development all the way through the Sermon on the Mount. Matthew 7:6 is the only verse where there is at first some difficulty seeing where it fits in. It goes on to a slightly different point but one closely connected to verses 1-5. Verses 1-5 had to do with judging fellow disciples. Now verse 6 goes on to deal with what is likely to happen if the hypocritical disciple tries to impose his perfectionism on outsiders.

A fellow disciple is likely to judge us in the way we judge him. An outsider will be more aggressive altogether. Let the hypocritical disciple try to impose his inconsistent and hypocritical criticism on the 'dogs and pigs' who have no interest in living a godly life anyway, and see what response he will get! His pearls of moral analysis will be trodden down with scorn, and his offers of help with the speck of dust will be received with violent indignation. 'Who are you to turn to me with your advice? What about this ... and that ... and this ... in your life?' The pigs and dogs of this world – who do indeed need help – have no time for the Christian with an obvious plank of wood in his eye. 'What is holy' refers to the gospel.

This is the most searching, challenging and humbling part of the Sermon on the Mount, especially for preachers and theologians and moral analysts! How easily self-righteousness grips us. How much criticism and how little appreciation! Self-righteousness exposes all things, is sceptical of all things, is suspicious of all things, slanders all things, and endures nothing! It criticizes specks and tolerates logs. It speaks when it has no right to speak. It interferes when the matter has nothing to do with us. It gets irritated with people and easily denounces them. Like Eli criticizing Hannah for drunkenness (1 Sam. 1:14), it passes judgment despite abysmal ignorance of the facts. God have mercy upon us. We need it. The opposite is love, love which bears all things, believes all things, hopes all things, endures all things.

26. Asking and Receiving
(Matthew 7:7-11)

The Sermon on the Mount is set out in a very logical manner. It is a mistake to think of it as a jumble of thoughts heaped together. Anyone who is actually wanting to live this Sermon on the Mount will feel that these verses are exactly in their right position. The Sermon is coming towards its end. Jesus comes to his great conclusion in Matthew 7:12 and appeals to us to actually live this life (7:13-14). We must beware of false prophets who will lead us into any different kind of life (7:15-23). Wisdom is a matter of building one's life on Jesus (7:24-27). But before we come to this conclusion in 7:12-27, it is surely natural that we should feel the need of his saying more about prayer. We feel the need of prayer at this point, after all that Jesus has said so far. The beatitudes made us feel that we have a long way to go in living the godly life (5:2-16), the 'law of Christ' in 5:17-48 was a very different kind of law from what we might expect and it demanded such a high standard of purity and love and freedom from anger. The call to live righteously before God and to live in freedom from covetousness and worry (6:1-34) were also greatly challenging. Now Jesus has asked us to break away from a judgmental attitude (7:1-6). At this point we might almost be in despair. It is a wonderful life that Jesus has portrayed but will it ever be possible for any of us to actually live it? Matthew 7:7 comes in at that point: 'Ask and it shall be given to you!' There is no reason why we should not live this life of the Sermon on the Mount. Every need, every grace, will be supplied to those who ask.

1. Prayer has a lot of asking in it. Jesus insists on the great willingness of God to hear and answer our requests. *Ask and it shall be given to you; seek and you will find; knock and the door will be opened to you* (7:7). There is a lot of asking in the stories of Jesus' life. He received many requests from needy people in Israel. These are virtually prayers to Jesus or to God through Jesus. The leper (Matt. 8:2; Mark 1:40) requested cleaning. The centurion wanted a miracle for his servant (Matt. 8:5-6). The sick and demonized people of Matthew 8:16 (Mark 1:32-33) were brought in the hope that they would be healed and delivered. The disciples in peril on the sea called for rescue (Matt. 8:25; Mark 4:38). The friends of a paralytic asked for help (Matt. 9:2; Mark 2:3). The synagogue official pleaded for his daughter (Matt. 9:18; Mark 5:22-23) and a woman looked for healing of a haemorrhage (Matt. 9:20-21; Mark 5:25-28). Two blind men asked for sight (Matt. 9:27; Mark 10:51) and a dumb man was brought for deliverance (Matt. 9:32). On another occasion a man was brought who was both blind and dumb (Matt. 12:22). The Syro-Phoenician woman had a request for her daughter

(Matt. 15:22, 25, 27; Mark 7:25, 28). The deaf and dumb man of Mark 7:32 is brought to him. A man pleads that the disciples will heal his sick son (Matt. 17:14-20; Mark 9:14-29). Two blind men near Jericho asked for their sight (Matt. 20:30; Mark 10:46-52).[28] In Mark's Gospel it is made clear that the healing of Peter's mother-in-law came in answer to an appeal for help (Mark 1:30). In connection with these people the value of their faith is emphasized (Matt. 8:10, 26; 9:2, 22, 28-29; 14:31; 15:28; 17:20; Mark 2:5; 4:40; 5:34; 10:52). Matthew 17:20 also reminds that lack of faith can result in weakness in prayer.[29] Faith is emphasized in connection with the cursing of the fig-tree (Matt. 21:21-22). Sometimes (Matt. 4:24; 14:35 and 15:30; Mark 3:7,8; 6:55, 56) mention is made of the vast numbers of sick people who came to Jesus or who were brought to him.

Jesus himself came close to receiving prayer to himself. On one occasion someone knelt before him, almost as if in worship (Matt. 9:18). The same thing happened again when Jesus controlled the wind and the waves of the sea (14:33). Certainly now that Jesus is enthroned at the right hand of the Father we may be sure he receives our prayers and hands them to his Father.

The requests that were brought to Jesus were mainly requests for healings of one kind or another. There are also requests for understanding or for explanation (Matt. 9:14; 13:36; 18:1; Mark 2:18) and Peter's request for a word of command that he should walk on the sea and then

---

28. The references listed here together with those in chapter 17 include all the main material in Matthew's Gospel in connection with prayer. I doubt whether Matthew 8:28-34 should be put in this list.

29. Matthew 17:21 is not in the best manuscripts.

for rescue when his faith was wavering (14:28-30). The Zebedee family requested a privileged position in God's kingdom (Matt. 20:20-28; Mark 10:35-45). Every one of these requests was received sympathetically. Prayer includes a lot of straightforward asking! Often Christians do not have because they do not ask (Jas. 4:2). True, there are other things in prayer besides asking: adoration and meditation and confession. But asking is part of prayer too, and a major part. Let your requests be known, said Paul (Phil. 4:6).

2. The answer to asking is receiving. *For everyone who asks receives; everyone who seeks finds; and to everyone who knocks the door will be opened* (7:8). Prayer will get an answer. It might not be exactly in the form we want; God has the right to modify the answers to prayer that we seek. But in one way or another prayer will always be answered. Jesus said, 'Ask and you shall receive' (John 16:24). When we are praying in the will of God, God will answer and the answer will be good.

3. Prayer may grow. One gets the impression of increasing intensity in these commands of Jesus. 'Ask ... seek ... knock ...'. Are they three ways of saying the same thing? I do not think so. Seeking is more than asking. When one asks and no answer seems to come, one seeks. One looks more persistently for the answer. When seeking seems to produce no answer, one gets more desperate and begins to knock at the door urgently. There is progress here. It is Jesus' way of telling us to persevere if the answer to prayer does not come speedily.

4. Jesus gives encouraging promises to the person who prays. '*Everyone who asks receives ... the door will be opened*' (7:8). There are many promises of this kind in Scripture. 'You will pray ... and I will listen' (Jer. 29:12), says God to his people. Whatever you ask in prayer, believing, you will receive (Matt. 21:22).

5. Jesus promises that our praying will be appropriately answered. *Or what man is there among you who, when his son asks for a loaf, will give him a stone? (7:9) Or if he asks for a fish, will he give him a snake? (7:10) If you then who are evil know how to give good gifts to your children, how much more will your Father in heaven give good things to those who ask him? (7:11).*

Jesus' final encouragement is that when we seek God in prayer, we may be sure that his way of treating us will be straightforward, generous and kind. (In passing, Jesus asserts the universal sinfulness of the human race; and he asserts his own freedom from sin: '*you* who are evil'). A loaf and a stone looked similar in Jesus' day. Fish were abundant in the area of the Sea of Galilee; no parent would ill-treat his child so badly as to give an eel-like snake instead! The point is: God's answers will be good answers. His answers to our prayers will be 'good things' – but not always 100% identical to what we asked for. A parent does not always give a child exactly what is requested; sometimes a *good* substitute will be given instead. A wicked substitute (a stone, a snake) is inconceivable, even in foolish and neglectful parents.

Verses 9-11 make it clear that verses 7-8 are not an offer of getting anything and everything we might want.

Sometimes when we pray, we thank God for answering our prayers. But sometimes as we pray we look back over our lives and there are some prayers we prayed that we thank God for *not* answering. We prayed and God did something different – but he never gave us stones or snakes. Sometimes without realizing it we were asking for a stone and God gave us bread!

What an encouragement to prayer these verses are, and how much we need them! 'Getting ourselves to the point of praying' – said the great and wise Martin Luther – 'causes us distress and anguish, and this requires the greatest skill.' The devil 'snatches us from our prayer and makes us so dizzy that we do not even think of praying. By the time you begin praying you have already tortured yourself half to death.' Satan is 'well aware of what prayer achieves and can do. That is why he creates so many obstacles and disturbances, to keep you from getting around to it at all.'[30]

Friendship with God involves speaking to him, responding back to what he says to us. We talk to him in many ways. Our worship is our expressing our enjoyment of him and of his character and his ways with us. We are given the Holy Spirit to help us in thanksgiving. We get into the habit of committing our ways to him. Day by day we put to him specific petitions for our needs. Often we have to supplicate him, that is to cast ourselves on his mercy. We also intercede for others. God lays burdens upon us that we take when we pray for the needs of friends and family and of our kinsmen and our nation. Part of talking to God is confession of sin, when the Spirit convicts

---

30. See Luther, *Sermon*, p.232.

us and leads us to acknowledge what he has said to us by way of rebuke. There are also forms of prayer that are not rational and logical. There are groanings that cannot be uttered and there is the gift of tongues.

Pray! says the Bible. Call to me and I will answer you (Jer. 33:3). People ought always to pray (Luke 18:1). Pray constantly (1 Thess. 5:17). Devote yourself to prayer (Col. 4:2). Make your requests known (Phil. 4:6). Pray at all times in the Spirit (Eph. 6:18).

27. A Rule of Thumb
(Matthew 7:12)

Jesus now comes to his conclusion and climax. The rest of the sermon adds no new commands. *So then, what you want people to do for you, you do that also for them, for this is the law and the prophets* (7:12). It puts in a nutshell everything he has been saying from Matthew 5:3 to Matthew 7:11. As Luther put it, he 'wraps it up in a little package where it can all be found.'[31] This is the most praised – but not the most practised – of all the sayings of Jesus. All sorts of people admire it and because they admire it they think that they admire the Sermon on the Mount (but generally they do not notice how much Jesus draws attention to himself in this sermon). There are many similar sayings of the world's moral teachers that sound similar to what Jesus said, but Jesus was the first to put this 'golden rule' positively. Many other moral teachers have put it negatively: 'Do *not* do to others what you do *not* want

---

31. See Luther, *Sermon,* p.235.

them to do to you.' Jesus was unique in being the first to put the principle positively.

It gives us a little one-sentence rule-of-thumb that will give us what to do in a thousand complicated situations: what you want people to do for you, you do that also for them.

1. It assumes that the disciples' self-love is not completely wrong. We are all self-centred. Even people who call others self-centred are themselves self-centred! Jesus is, of course, giving this principle only to his disciples. To people he has described as the salt of the earth and the light of the world, he says, 'You do that ... for them.' This saying involves another one: 'You shall love your neighbour as yourself.' Jesus takes it for granted that his disciples have a loving concern for themselves and will be quite skilful at knowing what would be good for themselves. The Bible never *commands* us to love ourselves, and it speaks of a wrong kind of self-love (2 Tim. 3:2). Yet Scripture assumes that people do love themselves and they are not completely condemned for doing so. There is a kind of self-respect and self-concern that is good and right. It only becomes sin when it becomes too extreme and becomes self-love at the expense of suffering in the lives of other people. But self-love is not completely wrong, and when we have a low self-image it makes us treat other people badly. We need a sense of dignity, a feeling that our life is worthwhile. We are sinners, but we are not garbage, and we are redeemable. We should want to be rightly treated; Jesus assumes that disciples will have this good and right instinct. We treat others well because we want to be well-treated ourselves.

171

A RULE OF THUMB

2. It is short and easy to remember – or it ought to be! If you keep this 'Golden Rule' in mind 'you are your own Bible', as Luther said.[32] You do not need a book of rulings about what to say or do in difficult situations.

3. It is comprehensive. There is no situation we shall ever find ourselves in where this little ruling will not give guidance. It takes us by the hand and leads us in the right direction in a thousand-and-one situations. It will give us answers in complicated situations. It will help us in a difficult marriage. It will direct us when we have rebellious children. It will guide us when we are persecuted and under pressure.

4. It leads us into asking the right questions. It is practical. You talk to yourself and ask yourself a few questions: What is it that hurts me? What do I dislike? What upsets me? What brings out the worst in me? What causes me distress and suffering? That gives me what to avoid, what not to do, in a thousand different relationships.

Then one asks more positive questions: What is it that I like? What do I like being done to me and for me? What encourages me, pleases me, helps me? What do I like to be said about me? What do I like people to say to me?

When I am in the wrong and have made a bad mistake what would I like others to do about it?

Then I know how to treat others: *what you want people to do for you, you do that also for them*. Jesus' little 'Golden Rule' focuses on the spirit, the heart, the attitude. It allows flexibility. It leads me in the direction of that

32. See Luther, *Sermon,* p.236.

172

true righteousness which is supremely a matter of knowing how to show love to everyone everywhere.

5. It provides answers. The answers come thick and fast. I like people to be nice to me; then I must be nice to others. I don't like it when people put me down or criticize me needlessly; then I must not put anyone down or criticize them needlessly. When I am completely wrong I hope people won't squash me into the ground and I hope they will let me get right again without being moralized and humiliated. That tells me how to handle the other person when he or she is completely wrong. It means that Jesus will have to help me not to crush that other person into the ground and I must let them get right again without my moralizing them or humiliating them. What I want people to do for me, I must do for them.

What do I like? I like people to be nice to me even when they know I am not perfect. If they wait until I am perfect before they are nice to me, they'll wait for ever. But then, that tells me something about how to relate to them. If I wait until others are perfect before I am nice to them, I will have to wait for ever! I had better start being nice, despite how horrid they are to me. After all, that's how God treats me.

What do I like? I like people to be communicative and to tell me what is going on, keeping me well-informed. I like people to greet me and say 'hello' when they see me, and say something before they take their leave. I like them to answer letters straightaway and not keep me wondering what is happening. I like them to sympathize with my impatience and know that I am a fast-mover and fast-talker

173

and (sometimes but not always) a fast thinker and do everything in a hurry! I like them to tell me their plans as early as possible, not as late as possible. I like their talk to be clear and straightforward without hints and obscurity and evasiveness and excuses. But then all of this rebounds back in my direction. God says to me: *So then, what you want people to do for you, you do that also for them.*

What do I like? I like people to 'flow' with me and let me be myself. So God says to me: *what you want people to do for you, you do that also for them.* You 'flow' with them and let them be themselves. Let them be slow thinkers! Slow-movers! That is the way you would want to be treated if you were made the way they were made.

What do I like? I like to be understood – even when I am difficult to be understood! I'll talk for half-an-hour if necessary to get someone to understand my point! But then what I like bounces back to me. I had better be ready to listen for half-an-hour to those I ought to understand.

I know what I like. But what do you like? I'll give you equal time! What you want people to do for you, you do that also for them.

6. It demands action. The negative version ('Do not do to others what you do not want them to do to you') can often be kept by doing nothing! It is a protection against others' retaliating when we do them wrong. If we do them no harm they might do us no harm. But Jesus' positive version ('what you want people to do for you, you do that also for them') demands that we do something. The negative version is not to be despised. If we control our tongues and do not insult others with the abuse that we ourselves

would not like to receive, then we have achieved something. But the positive version goes even further. It positively overcomes evil with good. It is supernatural; only the disciples of Jesus can do it, and they can only do it when the Holy Spirit is working within them. Everyone who lives this way is born of God and knows God.

7. It fulfils God's central purpose in the history of salvation. What is salvation all about? What has God been seeking to do during the many centuries of human history since the day Adam and Eve first sinned? This is it! 'This is the law and the prophets.' This is what God has always been seeking to do: to bring into being a kingdom of love! 'This is the message that you heard from the beginning' (1 John 3:11). From the earliest day God has been seeking to 'crush the head of the snake' – but the snake did more than one thing. It introduced rebellion against God, and unbelief, but the snake also introduced lovelessness into the world. The story of the fall in the garden is followed by the story of Cain and Abel. The introduction of rebellion against God was the introduction of hate among humans. When God introduced the Mosaic law it was taking a further step in the direction of love. The law was never perfect. It was negative rather than positive. But it was a step in the right direction. It was good and spiritual because it took one nation, the nation of Israel, in the direction of salvation and the restoration of love. The Mosaic epoch has ended but we are fulfilling its goal if we become people of love, people who when they recall what they want people to do for them, they do that also for others. This is the gist of the prophetic message: the abolition of hatred towards God

175

and men, the introduction of the kingdom of love in and through our Lord Jesus Christ.

Look at God's graciousness to you. Look at your own unworthiness and wickedness. Then look at the needs of others with sympathy and compassion, and what you want people to do for you, you do that also for them. The reason that the Son of God appeared was that he might undo the story of Adam's fall – and then undo the story of Cain and Abel, and bring into being a kingdom of love.

28. A Time for Decision
(Matthew 7:13-14)

From now to the end of his Sermon on the Mount Jesus will be calling for response to what he has said. He begins with an appeal to 'enter the kingdom'. The idea of 'entering the kingdom' is used in at least three different ways in the Bible. It is a mistake to think that it always means 'getting saved' or 'becoming a Christian'. As I have urged before, the Sermon on the Mount was addressed to disciples; it assumes that those who are listening are the salt of the earth and the light of the world. This appeal to 'enter the kingdom' is not an appeal to experience the first stage of salvation; it is not an appeal for new birth or for one's first repentance and faith. Rather it is an appeal that these disciples listening to Jesus will press on into a rich experience of the power of God's kingdom in their lives.

Jesus speaks both of 'ways' and of 'gates'. Entering the kingdom of God is like travelling on a pathway and coming to a junction where you have to pass through one

of two gates. The person who is *already* a disciple is faced
with two pathways through life. The fact that he is already
a disciple does not mean that he will automatically follow
the right way. Grace reigns over us, but not in such a way
as to remove our own choices and decisions. Grace enables
us to make good decisions, but it does not force them upon
us and we are still conscious of having to make real and
sometimes painful choices.

One could put it like this (although I am somewhat over-
pressing Jesus' illustration in order to clarify one point).
There is the kind of person who is not a disciple of Jesus
at all. He is already on a road travelling to destruction. No
'gate' appears before him or her. Such a person is
'condemned already' (John 3:18). The anger of God abides
on him (John 3:36).

But when a person puts faith in Jesus Christ, at that
point the road divides into two and two gates appear. From
that point on there is the possibility of walking in one of
two different directions. These disciples listening to the
Sermon on the Mount have already trusted in Jesus; they
already have such faith in him that they have left the towns
and villages of Galilee and have come away to a hillside
to listen to further teaching from Jesus. Christians are
people who have already trusted in Jesus; they already
have faith in Jesus and are willing to listen to him. The
Sermon on the Mount is addressed to such people.

Even after you have come to faith in Jesus, there are
still decisions that have to be made. The way ahead of
you might bring you life; it might bring you ruination. It
all depends on what decisions you make. Jesus is your
Saviour. He helps you make right decisions, but you do

177

need to make those right decisions. Even though you have left the world and are on a hillside with Jesus, it is still possible to make wrong decisions which will bring devastation and disaster to your life. What you do with the future of your life will ruin you or bless you.

1. A decision has to be made. Jesus says *Enter in through the narrow gate....* You are walking down a broad pathway. Then there appears ahead of you a fork in the road. The pathway divides into two. If you are to keep moving down the road you have to make a decision. Are you going to go down the one road or down the other? This is the position of the person who has come to faith in Jesus. It gives him freedom to make a choice between two ways of walking through life.

Someone might want to say, 'It is inevitable that the disciple will make the right decision. Once saved, always saved!' Well, I certainly believe in the Christian's security, but this does not mean that a Christian can never make a wrong decision. Holy living is not forced upon us; there is no violence done to us which drags us down the narrow way. The grace of God is ruling and reigning over our lives; God's grace will help us make the right decision but that decision will have to be made.

2. The easy choice has to be resisted. Jesus says: *Enter in through the narrow gate, because wide is the gate and broad is the pathway that leads to destruction, and many enter through it* (7:13). What is this broad way? It is the life that is the opposite of everything Jesus has been teaching in this sermon so far. It is the life that is self-

satisfied, not poor in spirit, always laughing at the things of God, but never made to mourn. It is the life that is aggressive rather than meek, that has no hunger or thirst for righteousness, that is unmerciful, impure, that destroys peace. It is the life that does not see God.

The vast majority of people live this way. Most people walking along the highway of life proceed along the highway without even noticing any gate! Even many disciples, though they have travelled up a hillside to hear Jesus, will nevertheless turn through a wrong gate.

This means that the Christian who wishes to 'enter the kingdom' and richly enjoy the working of God in his or her life, must get beyond the average Christian! Even the average Christian does not enter into everything that God has for us.

The broad way is the easy way. The decision to go the same way that most people go is not a difficult decision. It is made without any great struggle.

3. The more difficult choice has to be followed. At the point where most people are turning through a wide gate, you have to turn through the narrow gate! It is a lonely decision; you have to make it though no one comes with you. You have to turn through the narrow gate, even if you are the only one. *But small is the gate and narrow is the way that leads to life, and only a few find it* (7:14).

The narrow pathway that is followed when you turn through the narrow gate is the life of the Sermon on the Mount, the life that Jesus has been commending. It is the lifestyle of the beatitudes, of seeking to please God. It is the righteousness which far outstrips that of the scribes

179

and Pharisees, the life of victory over anger and adultery, that is free from foolish oath-taking, free from revenge, the life that shows love 'more than others'. It is keeping our eyes on God, laying up treasure in heaven rather than on earth, freeing ourselves from a judgmental spirit, treating others as we ourselves would like to be treated.

4. The two choices affect our destiny. One way is 'a pathway that leads to destruction'. In Matthew 7:13 Jesus is speaking mainly to disciples. There may be some in the crowd who have no faith in him, but his main concern is with those who are the salt of the earth and the light of the world. Both groups will be 'destroyed' in one way or another if they walk on the broad way.

The Greek word here is *apoleia* ('destruction, ruination'). It is worthy of fuller study, but all I can do here is give a few extracts from the relevant data. A*pollumi* ('destroy, kill, ruin') and *apoleia* ('destruction, ruination') get their meaning largely from the Old Testament, where *apollumi* is used to translate thirty-eight different Hebrew verbs meaning ruin, destroy, exterminate, wipe out, and suchlike.[33] I shall confine myself to the usage in Genesis, Matthew and Mark.

In Genesis, the supreme model in the Bible of God's punishment is the story of Sodom and Gomorrah. There, in the Greek Old Testament, our verb comes in Genesis 18:24, 28 (twice), 29, 30; 19:13, where it refers to God's 'destroying' Sodom and Gomorrah by fire and sulphur falling from heaven (19:24), so that the next day

---

33. The verbs are listed in Hatch & Redpath, *Concordance to the Septuagint* (1975 reprint), 1, p.136.

(19:27) nothing was left but the smoke of the land. The fire was an exterminating 'furnace' (Gen. 19:28); the extermination is called 'destroying' (Gen. 19:29). 'Destruction' from planet earth is the fate of the wicked.

This is a very important description of God's judgment and one which became definitive in the on-going story of the Bible. However there are much weaker uses of the word 'destroy' and 'destruction' than the one that appears in Genesis 19. In Genesis 20:4 (Greek Old Testament) it refers to the threat of the death which faces Abimelech and the 'ruination' of his people (see 20:3). In Genesis 35:4 it refers to the burying and removing of gods and earrings belonging to Jacob's family. The Greek text says 'Jacob destroyed them to this day' – meaning that the idolatrous utensils were made to be utterly lost, never to be seen again.[34]

In Matthew and Mark the verb comes twenty-nine times and the noun comes three times.[35] We can group the usage in the Gospels into five.

1. It may have a very weak meaning. Sometimes it refers only to something being damaged. Wineskins might be 'spoiled' (Matt. 9:17; Mark 2:22). Ointment might be 'wasted' (Matt. 26:8; Mark 14:4).

2. Sometimes it refers to something lost or mislaid or to a person who goes astray. In two occurrences in the Sermon on the Mount (5:29, 30) it means to 'lose' something. It is better to 'lose' something precious in this life than to face

---

34. The noun form *apoleia* is not found in Genesis.
35. Matthew 18:11 is not to be found in the best manuscripts.

punishment in Gehenna. Similarly we have reference to lost sheep (Matt. 10:6; 15:24), or a lost life (16:25, twice). When Jesus refers to 'losing one's soul' or 'losing one's life' (Matt. 10:39, twice; 16:25, twice; Mark 8:35, twice) the 'loss' includes something eternal. The second 'loss' in the verse (losing one's life for Jesus' sake) refers to self-surrender. The person who 'loses' his life in self-surrender does not 'lose' his reward (10:42). Mark 9:41 also refers to not losing one's reward.

3. It may refer to killing. We are coming to a stronger usage when the word means 'wipe out of existence *from life on earth*'. Herod 'destroyed' the children of Bethlehem (Matt. 2:13); the disciples once thought they were in danger of death (Matt. 8:25; Mark 4:38). The Pharisees took counsel how to 'destroy' – that is, 'kill' – Jesus (Matt. 12:14; Mark 3:6). The owner of the vineyard in Matthew 21 slaughters the wicked tenants (21:41; see also Mark 12:9). The angry king of Matthew 22:7 does something similar. 'Perishing by the sword' has the same idea (26:52). 'Destroying' Jesus comes in the same category (27:20; Mark 11:18). Death is in view in Mark 9:22.

4. It can be used of severe punishment for the Christian. It is this usage that is relevant to Matthew 7:13. It would be a mistake to think that when 'destroy' is used it always refers to eternal punishment. When Jesus says, 'It is not the will of my Father ... that one of these little ones should *perish*' (Matt. 18:14) the ruin involved is *not* what is traditionally thought of as 'eternal punishment'. Being thrown into eternal fire in Matthew 18:8 refers to a

'disciple' who suffers *something* of the retribution of God against sin.

David Pawson notices that most New Testament references to hell are addressed to disciples. 'Jesus warned his disciples of their own danger of being thrown into hell'. 'This challenge cannot be ignored ...', he says, and complains that both John Stott and Martyn Lloyd-Jones evade this datum of the New Testament.[36] He wants to deduce from this that Christians may lose their salvation. Pawson's observation concerning New Testament data is correct; it is true that most New Testament references to hell are addressed to disciples. But his deduction made from that fact is not necessary. We do not have to move into a doctrine of 'eternal insecurity' or 'once saved, maybe lost'. Rather this fact concerning the New Testament is part-and-parcel of the New Testament teaching concerning 'salvation through fire' (a term derived from 1 Cor. 3:15). The New Testament speaks of being '*hurt* by the second death' (Rev. 2:11) and of suffering loss at the judgment seat of Christ (1 Cor. 3:15) and of losing 'reward' in a fiery judgment (Heb. 10:26-31; note 'reward' in 10:35). It warns that when the judgment comes upon the 'sons of disobedience' (Eph. 5:6), the *righteous* who have had a share in the sins of the disobedient (Eph. 5:7) will forfeit 'inheritance in the kingdom' (Eph. 5:5) and experience the anger of God. There is no point in saying to Christians, 'Because of these things the wrath of God is coming' if that wrath cannot touch them *at all*. Yet 1 Corinthians 3:15 makes it crystal clear that the anger of God against

---

36. See D. Pawson, *The Road To Hell* (Hodder & Stoughton, 1992), pp.49, 97-98.

the sins of his people does not mean the undoing of their justification or the cancelling of their sonship or the removal of their new birth. It is justification, adoption and new birth which are eternally secure. However the hope of receiving 'inheritance' or the possibility of experiencing God's anger against the sins of his people are still open-ended matters.

In Paul's writings also (which I do not survey fully here) 'destroy' sometimes refers to a very severe loss but one not necessarily amounting to eternal perdition (see Rom. 14:15; 1 Cor. 8:11; 2 Cor. 4:9; 1 Tim. 6:9).

5. An even stronger use of the term is found in Matthew 10:28. Men can kill the body; God can kill body and soul. God's work of 'destroying' in Gehenna is parallel and analogous to what men do when they destroy someone on earth. The demons of Mark 1:24 feared this kind of 'destruction'.

In Matthew 7:13 Jesus is speaking mainly to disciples, although there may be some in the crowd who have no faith in him. Both groups will be 'destroyed' in one way or another if they walk on the broad way.

The other route is the more sweet for us to ponder. It is the 'way that leads to life'. The gift of God is life! It begins with life; it leads to more life; eventually the righteous 'go away ... into ... life' for ever (Matt. 25:46). This is the first time that 'life' is mentioned in Matthew's Gospel, but it is one of the great themes of the Bible. Jesus speaks of 'entering into life' (Matt. 18:8, 9; Mark 9:43, 45). The rich young ruler asked about having 'eternal life' (Matt. 19:16) which is the same as 'entering' into life (Matt.

19:17) or 'inheriting' eternal life (Matt. 19:29; Mark 10:17) or 'receiving' eternal life (Mark 10:30).

What is this 'life'? It is liveliness towards God; it is joy, energy in serving God, a sense of destiny, a joyful knowledge that the future holds nothing but good. The gate is a narrow one but it is 'a way that leads to life'.

29. False Prophets
(Matthew 7:15-20)

Jesus has been urging that the godly life has actually to be lived. His disciples must enter by a narrow gate and walk on a narrow way, and so experience the life of the kingdom of God (7:13-14). Matthew 7:15-20 now warns the disciples against false prophets. *Be on your guard against false prophets, who come to you dressed as sheep but inwardly they are greedy wolves* (7:15). In the flow of Jesus' words a false prophet is a person who claims to have a word from Jesus, yet who does not lead anyone into the life of the Sermon on the Mount.

1. False prophets come to us as we stand outside the narrow gate. Verses 13-14 have been urging us to enter the narrow gate. Verses 15-20 warn us that there will be people standing by the two gates urging us to enter not the narrow gate but the wide gate!

Who are these false prophets? We are asked to 'Be on guard'. The same language is used elsewhere of hypocrisy (6:1), of opponents of the gospel (10:17), of 'the leaven of scribes and Pharisees' (16:6, 11, 12) and of the Herodians

185

(Mark 8:15). Later (in Matt. 24:11-12) Jesus will warn against false prophets who encourage error, lawlessness and love-lessness. Other passages that warn against false prophets and false revelations are 1 John 4:1-3; 2 Peter 2:1.

2. The false prophet is difficult to recognize. What or who is the false prophet today? It is a difficult question to answer and Jesus expresses the difficulty. The false prophets come 'dressed as sheep'; they are not at first recognized at all, for they do not at all look like wolves.

It is partly a matter of teaching (see Matt. 16:12, 'Beware ... the teaching of the Pharisees and Sadducees ...'). Yet, since teaching and behaviour always affect each other, it is also a matter of the lifestyle the 'prophet' leads you into.

The false prophet is difficult to describe – but I shall try. He or she is a person who in one way or another fails to put to us a full and balanced gospel.

There is, for example, a man whose writings are on my bookshelf. He has in print seventeen little books of New Testament exposition. I have to say his writings are often stimulating, and I wish I could write as interestingly as he does. Yet he is a false prophet, undoubtedly. When you read more closely you discover he is always explaining away miracles. His expositions are expositions of morality, not expositions of the gospel. He does not believe in the deity of Christ, or the virgin birth of Jesus, or the physical return of Jesus – although you would have to be astute and observant to notice these things. Christians love his books! The reason is: the sheep's clothing is worn so skilfully! He is popular among Bible-believing people, yet the long-term drift of his work is to attack everything that Bible-believing Christians admire. Even expounding this very passage, he refers admiringly to Harry Emerson Fosdick (the American preacher who hated and ridiculed the gospel and was a false prophet if ever there was one!). It is surprising how false prophets can remove key aspects of the Christian faith from their central position – and yet be attentively listened to by Christian people and have their books displayed in Christian bookshops.

Yet perhaps this is not the most important example, because nowadays the false prophet is very 'evangelical', very 'Pentecostal'. The wolf dresses in the clothing of *today's* sheep. The wolves of yesterday and yester-year are now easier to recognize. The fangs of the wolf eventually get noticed! But just as it is easier to recognize yesterday's prophet than it is to recognize today's prophet, in the same way it is easier to recognize yesterday's *false* prophet than it is to recognize today's *false* prophet.

3. They are recognized by their fruit. *You shall know them by their fruits* – said Jesus (7:16a). The false prophet is someone who subtly twists the gospel so that the message of salvation through the blood of Jesus Christ, the Son of God, is no longer central. Godly living is no longer central. There is no narrow gate and no narrow way. Instead of focusing on sin and salvation and sanctification and serving God – the major themes of the Christian gospel – today's false prophet focuses on the profits of the gospel. His message tends to be about money and health and what a profitable thing it is to use 'faith' to get all these wonderful blessings! It is all dressed up in wonderful Christian

187

language and the poor sheep do not know they are deceived – not yet! The false prophet somehow omits the central message of salvation through the cross of the Lord Jesus Christ. He or she tends to *use* the Scriptures rather than *expound* the Scriptures.

And there is generally a lot of profit for the wolf! This is the real motive; *inwardly they are greedy wolves* (7:15). They do well financially and may even boast of how God is blessing them – but they are, of course, referring to money.

There is nothing new about this. The early Christian document called *The Didache*[37] also contains descriptions of the kind of false prophets that troubled the early church. 'If he comes in order to increase righteousness and the knowledge of the Lord, receive him as the Lord' says *Didache* 11:1, but 'If he asks for money he is a false prophet' (11:6). 'Anyone who speaks with a spiritual gift is not a prophet unless he have the behaviour of the Lord' (11:8). 'No prophet who orders a meal while speaking under the influence of a spiritual gift shall eat of that meal' (11:9). Another early Christian document, *The Shepherd of Hermas*,[38] contains similar warnings. 'The man who *seems* to have a spiritual gift exalts himself ...'. 'He lives

---

37. The *Didache* was discovered in 1875. It seems to come from the early second century AD. It does not have the atmosphere of power and life that we find in the New Testament, but it is important in giving us the principles of Christian conduct, and procedures in meetings, that were thought to be important in the second century.

38. The *Shepherd of Hermas* is the report of a series of visions. It dates from the AD 140s although parts of it may be earlier. Its teaching is not completely orthodox, since the writer thought Christians are able to live without sin after their baptism, and cannot be forgiven if they sin more than once after baptism.

188

in great luxury and accepts rewards for his prophesying. If he does not get them, he does not prophesy!' (*Shepherd of Hermas, Mandate* 11:12).

But the fruit is the important matter. Fruit takes time to appear. You cannot see how fruitful a tree will be the day after it is planted. The false prophet is *eventually* seen for what he is. In the long run it is not possible to deceive God's elect. The false prophet gets people off-centre from the central themes of the gospel. Eventually the promises held out by the false prophet are shown to be useless. The wealth does not come. The healing does not come. The 'deliverance' eventually leaves the person just as he was at the beginning! The 'blessings' promised come at the beginning, since Satan, the great Wolf, gives a little encouragement to the needy sheep! After a while the Christian discovers something has been lost. He or she has lost the joy of the Lord. The sense of God's blessing departs. You shall know them by their fruit!

4. The test is an inevitable one. It works with great accuracy. *Are grapes gathered from thorns or figs from thistles?* (7:16b) *So every good tree bears good fruit, but the bad tree bears evil fruit* (7:17). *A good tree cannot bear evil fruit and a bad tree cannot produce good fruit* (7:18). The false prophet *cannot* produce the godly life of the Christian. He is pointing people to the broad highway that leads to destruction. It is quite impossible that there should be any 'life' coming from God through his ministry. The false prophet is not pointing to 'the gate ... the way that leads to life'. No one gets spiritual liveliness towards God by taking notice of the message of the wolves.

5. False prophets will eventually be destroyed. Jesus repeats the message he himself had heard from John the Baptist. *Every tree that does not produce good fruit is cut down and thrown into the fire* (7:19). God hates sin and will judge it. Matthew has already let us know about the fire of God's wrath. He has mentioned earthly judgments: the deportation of 1:11, 12, 17; the sufferings of Israel mentioned in 2:17-18; the danger of being 'least in the kingdom' (5:19) or of failing to enjoy the blessing of the kingdom (5:20) or of forfeiting reward (6:1, 2, 5, 16) or of losing sense of God's forgiveness (6:15); the possibility of being judged by God and receiving back our own treatment of others (7:1). He has told of John's message about the anger of God against sin (3:7). John had used the imagery of chopping down a fruitless tree and casting it into the fire (3:10) and had warned of a coming baptism with fiery judgment as well as a baptism with the Spirit (3:11). When God comes – said John the Baptist – he comes to clear out sin and shovel it into a fire that cannot be put out and that burns up rubbish (3:12).

Jesus repeats John's message. He has warned of being unable to escape the judgment of God's court (5:22) and of suffering the fire of Gehenna (5:22). He has warned of being 'imprisoned' by God (5:25) until the last repayment is made (5:26). He has said to his disciples that it is better to lose their greatest privileges rather than have 'your entire body' in Gehenna (5:30). Now the same message is specially applied to the false prophet. He and his works and his words will all be consigned to fiery judgment (7:19). Jesus will disown them (7:23). Their ministry will be pronounced 'wicked' (7:23). Their house will collapse amidst rain and floods and winds (7:24-27).

Jesus' last sentence at this point is to his disciples: *So then you shall know them by their fruits* (7:20). He wants us to take responsibility in this matter and make sure that (by-passing the false prophet) we enter through the narrow gate.

30. Judgment Day
(Matthew 7:21-23)

The text flows straight on from 7:15-20. It deals with the experience of false prophets in the day of judgment.

> *Not everyone who says to me 'Lord, Lord' will enter the kingdom of heaven, but he who does the will of my Father in heaven* (7:21). *Many will say to me in that day, Lord, Lord, have we not prophesied in your name and driven out demons in your name and done many mighty works in your name?* (7:22) *And then I will say to them publicly, 'I never knew you. Depart from me, you who live wickedly'* (7:23).

This is not a passage about examining ourselves. There might be such passages elsewhere, but if so this is not one of them. Martyn Lloyd-Jones' superb (but not infallible) exposition says that Jesus speaks of the danger of self-deception 'not now in the false prophets, but in ourselves'.[39] Actually the text that we have before us quite clearly deals not with ourselves but exclusively with the false prophets! It is 'You shall know *them* by their fruits', not 'You shall know yourself by your fruits'. There is no change of subject. 'I will say to *them* publicly...'. Matthew

---

39. Lloyd-Jones, *Sermon*, 2, 223.

7:13-23 distinguishes clearly between 'you' and 'them', and the subject here is 'them'! Actually the New Testament does not have as much to say about 'the false professor' (that is, the 'imitation Christian') as the seventeenth-century Puritans thought. Their exposition of passages like these could be made more accurate.

1. Look first at the false prophet. He seems to be orthodox. He calls Jesus 'Lord'. This word often only means 'Sir' and is often not much more than a title of respect. But in the way Jesus uses it here it obviously means much more. This man has a high view of the lordship of Jesus.

This man is also zealous in the things of God. The repetition of the words 'Lord, Lord' gives the impression of zeal and enthusiasm.

He claims to have had the gift of prophesying – and the Lord does not dispute his claim. This is a mysterious subject but it seems that even unconverted people can have gifts of the Holy Spirit. Judas is an example. The disciples all went out two by two and they all came back saying, 'The demons are subject to us' (Luke 10:17). There is no hint that Judas stood out as any different from the others. When Jesus said, 'One of you will betray me', no one said, 'Is it Judas?' He was not distinguishable from the other eleven apostles. There is no reason to think that Judas was ever a child of God, yet he seems to have been used in ministry just as others were. Judases can be used by God.

The false prophet of Matthew 7 also claims to have done mighty works – and the Lord does not dispute his claim. It is possible (as Paul said in 1 Cor. 13:1-3) to have great gifts of speech and to have done mighty works and yet to be nothing at all in the kingdom of God.

The false prophet claims to have driven out demons. This too seems to be possible. Acts 19:13 tells of people who were without faith in Jesus but who used his name. False prophets may be able to perform such marvellous signs and wonders that even the very elect are almost deceived (see Matt. 24:24). 'Antichrist' himself will have miraculous powers (2 Thess. 2:9).

It is quite clear that a person does not have to be saved in order to speak for God. Balaam's ass should be the ultimate proof of that! God may use an unsaved person. The devil can produce imitations. And some people seem even to have certain unusual powers as part of ordinary human nature. Certainly one should not make great deductions about anyone's authenticity just because of any apparent powers of the miraculous he or she may have.

2. Look at Jesus' verdict. The false prophet will not enter the kingdom of heaven, either now or in the last day. He failed to do the will of God. He had no personal knowledge of Jesus. His punishment will involve prominent publicity. 'I will say to them *publicly* ...' It will involve terrible exposure. 'I never knew you,' Jesus will say, with the entire universe watching. Jesus will pronounce the false prophet to be a wicked person ('you who live wickedly'). His was not a case of backsliding. Jesus does not say, 'I knew you once but not now.' The man was always an intruder into the church of God. 'I never knew you,' Jesus will say. The false prophet's condemnation will involve eternal separation from Jesus, the Son of God. 'Depart from me,' Jesus will say.

We must remember that Jesus said these words about false prophets. It is a pity that anyone trusting Jesus should ever use them so as to scrutinize his own works to see whether his faith is genuine faith or not. I do not say that we should never scrutinize our works asking the question whether what we are doing is good or bad. But I do say we should not do so *in order to detect our own salvation*. Jesus makes these points, not to get his disciples to be full of doubts concerning their salvation, but to get them to be full of doubts concerning certain preachers they are listening to!

Equally I do not say we should never ask ourselves whether we have salvation, but the way to do so is not to ask about our works but to ask about our faith! The whole point of Matthew 7:21-24 is that one may produce very wonderful 'works' but it is not evidence of saving faith! Unsaved people who point to their own works generally *do* have assurance of salvation – but they are the people who are deluded. It is not believing that produces delusion! There is no way of becoming more deluded than to look at your 'good works' to prove your salvation. Consider the famous Pharisee of Luke 18. He thought he was praying. He honoured God's temple. He lived a moral life. He lived a disciplined life; he fasted. He lived a generous life; he tithed. Yet he was not accepted by God! He was such a 'good' man, and yet God would not accept him. No 'good works' of ours entitle us to stand before God. Our sanctification and our repentance is never sufficiently pure to entitle us to build our assurance on them. People who get 'assurance' this way are actually self-centred and self-deceived. Look at how much the Pharisee talked about 'himself'. 'I thank you that I am not like other people ... I fast ... I give tithes ...' When we have not yet seen our own sinfulness we talk about how righteous we are.

Your 'good works' will never be good enough. They only show that you need salvation. Don't talk about what good things you have done. Ask whether you do or do not believe that the Lord Jesus Christ is your only hope of salvation. To tell whether we believe the gospel or not is something that takes very little time. You either do or do not believe that Jesus is Lord and that God raised him from the dead. The false prophet of Matthew 7:21-23 did not have saving faith but he felt he could overthrow Jesus' judgment by talking about his good works! If faith leads to good works (and it does), then we ought to ask about faith and that is much easier than asking about good works! If it be said, 'But we have to ask whether our faith is genuine', I reply: faith is in itself assuring; faith is the opposite of doubt. How do we establish our faith by giving heed to our doubts? John Calvin's teaching at this point is much more trustworthy than some of his followers. Faith is 'confidence in the truth and power of God'; it is not intimidated by its own weaknesses and inconsistencies. It is 'accepting the promise of eternal salvation and the testimony of free adoption'.[40] It is not lost even when we are full of doubts. 'Men whose uncertainty over one particular affair disturbs and shakes them do not fall away, or lose their faith, nor are those branches tossing in the changing winds the sign of failure at the roots.'[41]

---

40. J. Calvin, *A Harmony of the Gospels Matthew, Mark and Luke* (Saint Andrews, 1972), p.15.
41. Ibid., p.16.

Calvin is quite clear that these words here in Matthew deal mainly with false prophets and hirelings who deceitfully work their way into the churches under the guise of being pastors, 'without the slightest mind for devotion.'[42] They are not having difficulties knowing whether they are genuine believers or not. They are phoney, and they know it. Judas himself could have told you he did not believe the gospel – if you could have got him to be honest! Jesus is not asking his disciples to doubt their salvation. As Calvin says, 'He is warning the faithful not to pay such shams any more respect than they deserve.'[43] As soon as the gospel begins to be successful there come 'even in the very ranks of the pastors' treacherous people who do not preach a full or accurate gospel. 'Often some of the worst impostors put on a fake holiness.'[44] They do not 'do the will of the Father', the first part of which is 'actually to believe upon Christ'.[45]

Christ's purpose here is to let his disciples know how serious is God's anger against anyone in the churches who corrupts the gospel. If there is any among the crowds of his disciples who are there not to listen in faith to Jesus' teaching but to sneak in among the disciples and earn a living with a message which has no 'narrow gate' in it, he lets them know what faces them at the judgment day.

Christ's purpose here is to let his disciples know they can sort out the true from the false if they pay careful attention to the 'fruit' of what is ministered. 'The faithful never lack the Spirit of discretion when they need it, as long as they have no self-confidence, but have in a real

---

42. Ibid, p.239.   43. Ibid, p.240.
44. Ibid, p.238.   45. Ibid, p.240.

sense said farewell to self, and entirely submit themselves to his direction.' 'All teachers need to be examined by the Word of God.'[46]

3. Let us look at Jesus himself. Jesus himself will be the judge in the last day. He speaks of his Father, but he is the one who does the judging. 'I will say ...' People who think that they admire the Sermon on the Mount often miss this. If they admire the Sermon on the Mount, may we ask, do they admire what Jesus says about himself? False prophets sometimes like the Sermon on the Mount but somehow they miss this bit. The remedy to all doubts and all questions is to see who Jesus is, hear his words, watch out for all that is fake and phoney – and build our house upon the Rock.

31. The Wise and the Foolish
(Matthew 7:24-27)

Jesus ends this lengthy piece of teaching with a parable (as he does also after blocks of teaching in Matt. 13:52; 18:21-35; 25:31-46). Jesus has spoken of 'you' (7:15-20), the disciples. He has spoken of 'them', the false prophets (7:21-23). Now he speaks to 'everyone'. He has in mind every person who hears his words, most of whom are his disciples but some of whom might now be outsiders. Matthew 5:1 spoke of Jesus' disciples, and most of this teaching on the hillside has assumed that his hearers are people who believe in him and are loyal to him. Yet when the teaching is finished, Matthew speaks of 'the multitudes'. It seems that the people nearby have attached

46. Ibid, p.238.

themselves to the disciples and have been listening on the edge of the crowd. So Jesus now speaks of 'everyone' who might hear him. *Therefore everyone who hears....*

Jesus puts his last appeal to us in the parable of the two houses.

> *Therefore everyone who hears these words of mine and does them will be compared to a wise man who built his house upon the rock (7:24). And the rain came down and the rivers overflowed and the winds blew and beat upon that house but it did not fall because it was established upon the rock (7:25). And everyone who hears these words of mine, and does not act upon them will be compared to a foolish man who built his house upon the sand (7:26). And the rain came down and the rivers overflowed and the winds blew, and they beat upon that house, and it fell and its fall was great (7:27).*

The two men both wanted to build houses. Life is like putting up a building. Everyone is building the house of his life. But the way in which the two men build is entirely different. One man is foolish. He builds his house on sand. This is the person who hears Jesus' words but does not take action as a result. The other builder is wiser and builds a house that will survive in a time of storm.

1. Our lives need a foundation. A wise house-builder makes sure he builds on a firm foundation. This is Jesus' parabolic way of referring to those who deliberately build on what they hear from him.

Living in this world may be compared to building a house. We are building something to live in, in the future. A time of storm and rain is likely to come upon us. We need shelter and protection ready for such a day. There are the rains of sorrows and the floods of troubles and the winds of adversity. The biggest storm of all history will

198

break about our heads when the Day of God's judgment comes upon the world and we have each to give an account of the deeds done in the body. We need a house of protection that will stand in such a day; and it needs a foundation.

2. The foolish man tried to build without a foundation. In Jesus' parable the 'foundation' is built as we hear the words of Jesus, and then firmly take action upon the basis of what we hear.

The first thing Jesus puts to us is a message about himself! He tells us that he is the Saviour and that there is no hope of salvation apart from knowing him. Even the most energetic doer of good deeds will have no salvation if he or she does not know Jesus Christ. But then there is more. Jesus says many things to us. He says again and again 'I say unto you'. He will talk to us in principles (as he does here in this Sermon on the Mount). He will press particular matters upon us by his Spirit. He will put a calling upon our lives, a sense of direction, a particular set of ways of serving God which are designed for the way God made us. He will talk to us about certain sins and ask us to deal with them. He will have much to say about love and forgiveness of others. He will ask us to persist in faith and endure in trials and withstand temptations.

But the foolish man does not take much notice of any of this. He is in a hurry to get the good things of life and does not bother with any foundation. He wants pleasures and blessings and would like the help of God to make sure he gets them. The foolish builder is too impatient and self-centred. He fails to build on a good foundation because of his carelessness and thoughtlessness. He does not want

199

to bother about ways of serving God and is too self-centred to think about loving ways or persisting in faith or withstanding temptations. He takes no notice of the guide-book; he refuses advice. 'I just want to get on building the house,' he says. 'Never mind all this talk about found-ations!' He is a fool. He wants a house but takes no trouble to have one that will endure.

3. The essence of wisdom consists of what one does with what one hears. The wise man is altogether different from the fool. Jesus speaks of two types of person. There is the person 'who hears these words of mine and does them' and there is the person 'who hears these words of mine, and does not do them'. Both people hear Jesus. There is no difference in them at that point. The crucial matter is not the hearing but the doing. One often hears someone saying, 'Now we have heard these things; let us go and put them into practice.' It is almost a traditional remark after some challenging preaching. Well, that is what is often said, but something drastic has to happen to us before we actually do put into practice what we hear.

The firm foundation is not hearing; it is doing. We do not build simply by believing the teaching. We are building on the rock when we actually take Jesus' words so seriously that they lead to changes and amendment in our lives. What will it take for it to happen? How do we make sure we have a good foundation for the storms of the future?

Realisation. We must accept that for much of the time we hear Jesus' voice and are satisfied with hearing. Somehow it makes us feel good just to hear God's Word. After hearing some good preaching we say, 'That was a blessing.' Actually Jesus said, 'If you know these things, blessed are you if you do them' (John 13:17). There are *two* ifs. The hearing is only a preliminary. There is no special blessing in hearing. The blessing comes afterwards if the word takes effect in our lives. Otherwise we are deluding ourselves. Hearing simply sets the conditions for blessing. We must realise our danger of getting past the first 'if' but failing at the second.

Retention. It is necessary for us to retain what we hear. James spoke of the person who looked in a mirror and forgot what he saw! Imagine a person looking in a mirror, seeing he needs to comb his hair, but then he forgets what he saw and goes out on his business with untidy hair! Some steps have to be taken to retain what we hear. It is not just a matter of taking notes of sermons. Preaching is often hindered by note-taking which turns the preaching into a rather academic affair. When the Holy Spirit really is at work, the note-takers forget to take notes! Turning preaching into writing has to be done in a different way than that, and changing churches into lecture halls with a university-like atmosphere and much scribbling of notes is not the answer. Someone has mentioned how the Jewish rabbis used to think study of the scriptures was the supremely important thing at the expense of other forms of action.[47] Well, study of the scriptures is important, but Jesus says nothing about studying the words of Jesus. Of course we have to do that, and I am doing it now! But the supreme thing in all our studies and all of our listening to preaching is to respond to what Jesus asks of us. Unless

47. See W.D. Davies & D.C. Allison, *A Critical and Exegetical Commentary on the Gospel According to Saint* Matthew, vol. 1 (Clark, 1988), p.720.

we see it this way we are moving towards disaster. Intellectualism is not the answer but we do need to make it a habit to firmly hold on to what God says to us. It will not happen unless we decide to make it happen.

Retaining what God says is a matter of making a different kind of note. I mean taking particular note of what God says to us to do. Then it must be made a matter of prayer and a matter of action.

Re-formation. We have to get into fixed habits of constantly re-forming our lives in the light of what God has said to us.

4. For a while the difference in buildings does not appear. When the sun is shining and the weather is nice the two men with the two houses are both enjoying living in their homes. Perhaps for a long time, all is well. Indeed the foolish man rather despises the wise man. 'That fellow spent so much time worrying about foundations,' he says. 'But my house got built more speedily than his house, and I am enjoying my house despite everything he said about foundations!' All is well for them both – as long as the sun shines.

5. A day comes when the strength of a building is tested. One day the sun is not shining so brightly. Soon dark thunder clouds form. Then the rain begins to pour down. The winds begin to blow. The test of a house is not what it is like when the sun is shining; it is what it is like when the storms come.

Soon the rains of distress and the storms of Satan's attacks and the winds of God's judgment will come upon us. Will our house stand? Will we continue to have a place of safety and peace when the hurricanes roar outside? The question is not: how are we enjoying life now? The question is: do we have protection for days of distress and judgment? It is only those who actually and literally obey our Lord Jesus Christ who will have peace amidst the storms. It will be terrible for people who have heard Jesus but never bothered to do anything about what he says and drift on the way they always have been. What will they do when adversity comes? What will they do when it is too late to do anything?

The wise man keeps close to Jesus and obeys everything Jesus says to him. The best place to begin is the Sermon on the Mount. Jesus is with me, and I am building that kind of life. His first instruction is that I have him as my Saviour. The storms will break at any moment. When 'upon life's billows I am tempest toss'd', when I am 'discouraged thinking all is lost' – I think again! I am within a house that the Lord Jesus Christ is helping me to build! For the moment the weather is quite sunny, but I can see some dark clouds in the distance. For myself, I smile at the storm, but I had best help my neighbours rebuild their houses. And maybe I should check those foundations.

32. An Amazing Preacher
(Matthew 7:28-8:1)

When the Sermon on the Mount is finished the people listening to it are astonished. They have never heard anything like it. Amazed reactions to this teaching have continued ever since.

1. The people are amazed at the content of the Sermon on the Mount. *And it happened that when Jesus has finished these words, the crowds were astonished at his teaching* (7:28). *For he was teaching them as a person having authority and not their scribes* (7:29). *And when he came down from the mountain great crowds followed him* (8:1).

The actual teaching itself is amazing. It is interesting, for it is full of picture language. It is playful and exaggerated: the picture of turning the other cheek is almost funny. It is full of everyday language (salt, coats, moths, rust, birds, flowers, grapes, fish, stones, trees, rain, wind, pigs – and much more). There is an extraordinary collection of very ordinary things mentioned in these chapters. The Sermon on the Mount is highly theological yet you would hardly notice. People who think there is no theology in the Sermon on the Mount have not read it properly – yet one can understand their mistake.

Most amazing of all is its spiritual content. It gets to the heart of what godliness and spirituality really consist. It does not have many rules or regulations, yet it focuses on attitudes (meekness, peaceableness), on inner freedom (from greed, from pride, from anxiety). It deals with our love-lessness, our judgmental attitudes, our parading religiosity. It tells us how to relate to God's old law, how to live before God, how to regard his judgment. Was there ever a collection of such vital matters so sweepingly expounded in so short a space? Who ever thought of the 'Golden Rule' (7:12) before Jesus said it? A few came near, but who ever put it so positively, so searchingly, as Jesus did? For those who have eyes to see, the Sermon on the Mount is one of the greatest proofs that Jesus is who he says he is.

2. The people are amazed at the manner in which Jesus spoke. Here is this young man in his thirties, a carpenter's son from the despised area of Galilee. Yet he does not show the slightest timidity or uncertainty; he speaks as if he is totally sure that what he says is from God. He is not reading an essay, as some modern preachers do. He is not sharing his thoughts about current Israelite politics. There are no literary allusions to what learned scholars are currently reading. It is all so utterly different from what the people heard from the scribes of the synagogues. The scribes liked to parade their learning. They would quote the learned authorities. 'Rabbi So-and-so said this; and Rabbi Such-and-such said that'. They would give short little essays that were digests of what scholarly people were currently saying.

But this young man in his thirties preached in a way that was so different from the scribes. He spoke with such authority. It was not the authority of having studied a lot; it was the authority of having a spiritual understanding that came from God. Jesus knew that what he was saying was from God. The crowds could see it and it astonished them.

But it was not simply the authority of knowing one has a message from God. There was an added element. There was a sense of the Holy Spirit's authority. The Holy Spirit had come down upon the Lord Jesus Christ at the time of his baptism in the River Jordan. From that point on there was a power resting upon him that was more than natural. People could feel it. When he spoke, there was a sense of piercing directness in what he said. When Peter received the Holy Spirit on the day of Pentecost it immediately transformed his preaching. It immediately created a new style of speaking with authority. People listened as never before. It cut them to the heart. They cried out, 'Men and brothers, what shall we do?' It was this kind of authority that could be felt in Jesus long before anyone felt it in the apostle Peter. Jesus had already had his own day of Pentecost! It led immediately to authority in his preaching.

3. The people are amazed at Jesus' manner of speaking of himself. The most surprising thing of all in the Sermon on the Mount is the way in which Jesus draws attention to himself. These disciples are 'his disciples' (5:1). He talks to them as One who is their Lord. He speaks quite dogmatically about knowing what is needed for anyone to 'see God' (5:8). He says there is a blessing for anyone who is persecuted 'on account of me' (5:11). Jesus himself is central in this 'sermon'. The person to be congratulated is the person who is identified with Jesus.

Then he tells them why he came to this world. He says, 'I have come to fulfil the Scriptures' (5:17). 'Come' from where? Not 'come' from Galilee or Jerusalem. Rather he tells them why he has 'come' into this world, 'come' from God himself. He has come into this world to fulfil the entire Scriptures, and now that he has come and has fulfilled them, he feels free to modify and carry forward God's instructions concerning righteousness. He fulfils every dot and comma of the entire Old Testament, but now he carries their programme forward a stage further! He claims that the Old Testament is all about him, but now he is going to speak of things that go beyond the Old Testament. The law has a programme of action which has to be fulfilled and Jesus is the one who will accomplish its purpose. The law is not abolished but it is transcended by Jesus himself. Jesus is giving his own commands which outstrip and outclass the equivalent commands in the Mosaic law. He introduces a requirement of love which puts the sixth commandment in the shade. He will cancel some provisions allowed in the law. He will allow some things forbidden by the law. It was quite clear to the people listening to Jesus that these commands of Jesus are Jesus' *own* commands. Who does Jesus think he is? Again and again he says, 'I say to you...' He speaks as one who knows who will go to Gehenna, who will have their sins forgiven, who can talk to God and how. He claims to know about the narrow pathway to heaven and the small gate that is the starting-point of the way.

Most amazingly of all, he claims that he will be the judge on the Day of Judgment. 'Not everyone who says to me "Lord, Lord" will enter... have we not prophesied in *your* name and driven out demons in *your* name and done many mighty works in *your* name?' Jesus says, 'I will say to them publicly, "I never knew you. Depart from me..."'
It is all amazingly self-centred. Either Jesus is insane, the most amazingly ego-centric madman there ever was. Or he is a great charlatan. Or he is the divine Messiah sent from God! There can be no half-and-half with this Lord Jesus Christ. His claims are so great you either have to accept them or reject them violently altogether.

It is noteworthy that Jesus speaks of 'your Father' and of 'my Father in heaven' but he never speaks of 'our Father' (except as a term the disciples should use together). He has a unique sonship. Their sonship and his sonship are not the same. He is claiming to be the unique Son of God.

Jesus asks everyone listening to build their lives personally on him. 'Everyone who hears these words of mine and does them ...'. When the final storm bursts upon the world, those who will survive are those who have built their lives on Jesus and his words. Even the most energetic doer of good deeds will have no salvation if he or she does not know Jesus Christ. Only those who actually and literally obey the Lord Jesus Christ will have any safety on that day.

Normally in preaching, the sermon is more important than the preacher, but this is a case where the Preacher is more important than the sermon, and the sermon has no meaning except in connection with the Preacher.

When Jesus returned from the hillside north of Galilee, 'great crowds followed him' (8:1). He had actually left the crowds (5:1), but wherever he went new crowds gathered around him. They recognized amazing authority, staggering claims.

The question is: what shall we do with this Sermon on the Mount? It is worthwhile our memorising large sections of it. One day a storm will break, the rain will pour down, the winds will blow, the floods will arise – and what we have done with the Sermon on the Mount will affect our life for ever and ever from that point onwards. The test in that day will be what we have done with the words of Jesus, because what we have done with the words of Jesus is what we have done with Jesus himself.

Now Jesus says 'I say unto you'; in the last day Jesus says, 'I will say to them publicly ...' He speaks to us now; he will speak to us then. What he says to us then depends on how we listen to him now.